THRIVING
IN
Strategies for the
LGBTQ+
Entrepreneur
BUSINESS

An Imprint for GracePoint Publishing (www.GracePointPublishing.com) in collaboration with Pride & Joy Publishing
GracePoint Matrix, LLC
624 S. Cascade Ave
Suite 201
Colorado Springs, CO 80903
www.GracePointMatrix.com
Email: Admin@GracePointMatrix.com
SAN # 991-6032

Library of Congress Control Number: *2021917357*
ISBN-13: (Paperback) – 978-1-951694-78-4
eISBN: (eBook) - 978-1-951694-77-7

Books may be purchased for educational, business, or sales promotional use.
For bulk order requests and price schedule contact:
Orders@GracePointPublishing.com

CONTENTS

Want to Read More?   v
Foreword   vii
Joe DiPasquale   xiii

1. Live Your Truth to Find Your Life Worth Living   1
   Dean Rasmussen   7
2. A Brief Field Guide to Queer Storytelling   9
   Braidyn Browning   17
3. Intentional Empathy   19
   Anna Miller   29
4. Empathic Leadership   31
   Josh Miller   39
5. From Burn Out to Glow Up   41
   Takeyla Benton   53
6. Intuition in Business   54
   Harris Eddie Hill   63
7. The Power of OPA!   65
   Elena Joy Thurston   75
8. Bringing People Together, One Book at a Time   77
   Lisa B. Forman   85
9. (LGBTQ+) Networking as Your Secret Weapon   87
   Rocio Sanchez   95
10. Marketing Through Authenticity   97
    Amanda Swiger   103
11. Reframing Doubt   105
    Noopur Shah   113
12. Pitching with Authenticity, Clarity, and Style   115
    JD Schramm   123
13. Finding the Real You   125
    Bree Pear   133
14. The Audacity to Think Bigger   135
    Bastian Dziuk   142

A Note to Our Readers   145
Find out More   147
Footnotes   149

WANT TO READ MORE?

For more great books, please visit Pride & Joy Publishing online at
https://gracepointpublishing.com/pride-and-joy-publishing

PRIDE & JOY
publishing

FOREWORD

JOE DIPASQUALE

How far we've come! When I first co-founded StartOut in 2009, a non-profit to foster and develop entrepreneurship in the LGBTQ community, there were no openly LGBTQ CEOs of Fortune 500 companies. Other groups were certainly underrepresented as well: only 5% were women, and only 1% were Black. But, in the last ten years, our LGBT community went from zero openly LGBTQ CEOs of Fortune 500 companies to several: Tim Cook of Apple, who came out publicly in 2014 after being named CEO; Beth Ford of Land O'Lakes, Jeff Gennette of Macy's, and Jim Fitterling of Dow Chemical Company.

Yet, how far we must go. This takes our representation to 0.8% amongst the highest echelons of business leadership, while the Gallup poll's 2020 update on lesbian, gay, bisexual, or transgender identification found 5.6% of U.S. adults identifying as LGBTQ. To be fairly represented, there would need to be 7x more openly LGBTQ CEOs of Fortune 500 companies.

While there are some promising statistics—LGBTQ employees who make it into senior management are much more likely to be out than closeted—there are many more that show the challenges. The unemployment rate for the LGBTQ community is

13 percent compared to 9 percent of non-LGBTQ Americans; and 53 percent report that discrimination negatively affects their work environment. Twenty-seven percent of transgender people who held or applied for a job in the last year reported being fired, not hired, or denied a promotion due to their gender identity. The transgender unemployment rate is 3x higher than the national average.[1]

One of the wonderful things about entrepreneurs is that we are widely considered the engine of economic development. Small businesses created by entrepreneurs are disproportionately responsible for job growth. They create more than 1.5 million jobs annually in the United States, which translates to 64 percent of total new job growth[2]. But for disadvantaged communities, so often discriminated against in traditional work environments, is there also something necessary, even freeing, about being an entrepreneur?

Entrepreneurs can create their own job and environment; perhaps this is why disadvantaged communities have a history of choosing this path. In 2019, for example, immigrant entrepreneurs made up 21.7 percent of all business owners in the United States, despite making up just over 13.6 percent of the population.[3]

This book creates a special space for us to explore our own experiences as LGBTQ people Thriving in Business. If you're reading these pages, then perhaps you also recognize that we have something special and are grateful as I am to be connected on a deeper level: that of identity, and even community. When we bring this together with our passion for business and the practicality of commerce, we have a deep and meaningful bond that creates innumerable ways in which we can help each other. We may be underrepresented, but we can be a chosen family.

With LGBTQ resource groups abounding in even the most conservative companies and industries, this has certainly changed. For example, at a recent StartOut Awards, we honored R. Martin Chavez, former CFO of Goldman Sachs and openly LGBTQ, for his trailblazing work including starting Goldman's LGBTQ group.

We also honored Martine Rothblatt for her advancements in technology as creator of SiriusXM and CEO of United Therapeutics, and Jerome Guillen for his contributions as President of Heavy Duty Trucking at Tesla. These are just a few examples of the many amazing LGBTQ business leaders in the world today.

The LGBTQ community is large, and we would all be better served by recognizing not only the diversity but also the adversity that many have been through. While it's exciting to celebrate successes, we can also acknowledge the struggles of some in our community, and that we are empirically underrepresented.

The StartOut Pride Economic Impact Index, which is pioneering data on the impact of inclusion, shows that less than half a percent of all high-growth entrepreneurs in the ninety-nine metro areas studied self-identify as LGBTQ. It also shows that, with further inclusion and equality, the United States could have 427,950 more jobs created by LGBTQ entrepreneurs. This is why books like this are so needed; not only by our community, but the entire economy at the center of which is job growth and entrepreneurs who create those small businesses and jobs. For maximum prosperity in the world, LGBTQ entrepreneurs must have the skills to thrive.

Within the US, we see a great disparity in representation between places like the San Francisco Bay Area, which accounts for over 40 percent of venture capital raised by LGBTQ entrepreneurs in the US, and others. From the ninety-nine metro areas studied, over 70 percent did not have a single high-growth entrepreneur who openly identified as LGBTQ. Having these role models and this inclusivity would not only have created, by our estimates, 427,950 more jobs but would also have a compounding effect. As one study found, "[the] power of role models can be harnessed to increase role aspirants' motivation, reinforce their existing goals, and facilitate their adoption of new goals" (Morganroth, Ryan, and Peters 2015).

Outside the United States, we know that things can be even more difficult; it is illegal to be LGBTQ in sixty-three countries and punishable by death in six of them. At a recent StartOut event, I met a gay Malaysian entrepreneur seeking asylum and a way to operate his life and business without fear of harm.

Yet, too often, I have seen real struggles fall on deaf ears. This can especially be true in the business world, where "Victory has a hundred fathers, but defeat is an orphan" (JFK).

One of my own strategies for success is to acknowledge my own and others' unique paths, challenges, and even accomplishments in making it to where we are today.

Additionally, we must acknowledge that the opportunities available to one facet of our rainbow may not apply to another as we know. For example, the discrimination faced by trans people is much greater in general than many others. I believe that it is only through acknowledging these struggles that we can proceed to fully embrace strategies from which to overcome, thrive, and bring our unique gifts to the world.

To those who are struggling with discrimination: I acknowledge you. And I believe it's only from this place of acknowledgement that we can rise above and beyond and use our strengths to overcome and bring each of our unique gifts to the world.

Within this book, you'll find strategies and stories that, if applied, will help you thrive in business. These are tools and techniques that have already come in handy to me numerous times, from Braidyn's chapter on copywriting to the LGBTQ+ audience, to Takeyla's chapter on recovering from Corporate Burnout, to Josh's chapter on Empathetic Leadership.

Some of the best strategies I've engaged in in business are to authentically connect with others; to seek out mentors and those in a similar stage; and to pursue learning opportunities. When we incorporate ourselves holistically into our work, I truly believe we form stronger bonds. It is from this authenticity that you find others with whom you enjoy collaborating, doing business, and sharing a vision for the world. There are also many mentorship programs of various entrepreneurial and industry groups; Start-Out, for example, has hundreds of mentors and mentees through its program.

Learning is also at the center of this; there are numerous business incubators and classes that can be very helpful to learn how to create a business. Learning from others helps with structure and motivation: structure as key to creating a business with concrete goals and timelines; motivation as having others around you with whom you're pulling forward together.

Just as the world has rapidly grown and developed, to thrive as business leaders we must as well. In the last decade, openly LBGTQ business leaders have reached some of the highest echelons in business and paved the way for us. These successes are built on the bones of those who fought for our rights, those who went through a great, incomprehensible ordeal to bring us our freedom. Our success is their success too. So, choose your own adventure and direction, grab an LGBTQ mentor who's gone before you—perhaps through reading the pages of this book of wisdom—and thrive.

JOE DIPASQUALE

Joe DiPasquale is CEO of BitBull Capital, which manages diversified investment strategies in blockchain and cryptocurrencies.

Joe is also the founder of Regroup, the leading SaaS platform for mass notification, and co-founder of StartOut, a 501c3 that fosters entrepreneurship in the LGBTQ community. Business Insider named him one of the "23 Most Powerful LGBT+ People in Technology."

Joe is an expert in SaaS and enterprise technologies via

Regroup; entrepreneurship via StartOut; and the technology landscape via his hedge fund and venture capital investments. As an advisor for incubators including Stanford's StartX and the Founder Institute, he regularly evaluates technology businesses and focus areas of venture capitalists, including understanding Silicon Valley's technology pipeline and burgeoning investment verticals.

Previously, he worked in investment management, investment banking, technology, and strategy consulting at Deutsche Bank, Bain, and McKinsey. Joe completed his BA at Harvard University and MBA at Stanford University.

1

LIVE YOUR TRUTH TO FIND YOUR LIFE WORTH LIVING

"For every person who might reject you if you live your truth, there are ten others who will embrace you and welcome you home."

This quote by Marianne Williamson continues to pop up in my life in what I would consider the most unexpected of places and times. The impact of her words hits me like a ton of bricks **every. single. time.**

A few years ago, I met a boy named Carl. He was an adorable, chubby-cheeked, curly-haired three-year-old and he introduced himself to me at our local beach. He tore his t-shirt off leaving only navy-blue swim trunks with bright red lobsters printed on them and exclaimed, "From now on, you will call me Carl and I am a brother not a sister!"

Earlier that day, my preschooler insisted on wearing the lobster covered swim trunks belonging to his brother. At three years old, my innocent baby knew without any doubt that, although he was assigned female at birth, he was most definitely a boy. Aside from choosing a name other than Carl, he has not—for one second—doubted who he is since that moment.

If only his parent, who is more than three decades older and "apparently" wiser, could say the same.

At age twenty-one, I was married with two kids. Aside from being young, which, of course, I thought I wasn't, I was living the dream. Nice home, a spouse, two kids, a dog, and a cat. I was working at a job I enjoyed with people I liked.

When my kids were five and three, I found myself falling for a good friend of mine. Up until this point, I had no clue that I was gay. I had just turned twenty-five.

Looking back, I can see so many signs, but at the time I just assumed everyone thought and felt like I did about women! Honestly, what did I know, I still thought **I** was a woman.

I immediately ended my marriage and told my parents about my self-discovery. They didn't seem shocked; they also weren't overly supportive, but handled it in a "don't ask, don't tell" manner, which was typically how our family handled anything uncomfortable.

A year after I came out, I fell into a depression. I was dealing with trauma from my childhood, and I was living a very closeted gay life. Not living my truth and being my authentic self **nearly. ended. my. life**.

I was never bothered by being gay, but I struggled with the decision to stay closeted. The impact of years of self-abandonment had caught up with me and it was time to get some help.

Have you ever had a dream that you *chose* not to follow?

What about a want or a need within a relationship that you were too scared to address?

If those resonate with you, then I'm sure you can understand what I was going through. The toll of years of self-abandonment finally led me to therapy. I found a therapist that I clicked with, one who gave me that intuitive "this is the one" feeling. The work I did with her helped tremendously with my past trauma, but I still felt like something was missing.

The day after my twenty-sixth birthday, I decided *religion* was the thing that was missing from my life. It wasn't actually religion that I was seeking, but rather it was community. I just had no idea where to find community in my small conservative hometown—except at church.

In church, I found a sense of belonging there I had never before felt. It became my solace. The people became my family.

Except... I was still hiding a huge part of who I was, and it continued to wear on me.

Almost six months later, I met some people who attended another church, one of whom worked with my mom. I knew this woman had heard that I was gay and by this point I had come to understand how the church felt about homosexuality. She offered me a way to get "healing" from this "issue" that I had. Being gay had started to feel like it was causing more harm than good in my life, so I went for it!

The night of my deliverance came. I was going to be "healed" from homosexuality. I honestly don't remember what I was feeling. Hopefulness perhaps? I *do* know that when I left and returned home, I believed 100 percent that I had, in fact, been healed, and was no longer gay.

Over the next few years, I was busy with my new life as a single parent, homeschooling my two kids, getting heavily involved in church and more or less happily living life. But eventually I realized my kids would one day be gone from home and I might want to be with someone rather than live out the rest of my life alone. The thought of having more kids also intrigued me, so I decided to start dating men again.

When I was thirty-three, I met a man who was a good fit for what I thought I was looking for. At this point I still had total faith in the fact that I had been "healed" and was no longer gay. I also had no real concept at the time that same sex couples could have families and live the life I was trying to attain. I didn't know any queer couples or even have exposure to any healthy, happy, successful gay or lesbian couples. This kept me from believing that I could find success not only in a relationship, but also financially.

So, I got remarried and in less than three years had three more kids. During this time, rather than finding my own success and financial freedom, I helped my then-husband run his business.

A year later I had a miscarriage which I believe was a catalyst in finally choosing to live an authentic life.

Coming face to face with the knowledge of how quickly life can be over, forced my eyes to open to the detriment of burying a huge part of who I truly was.

The summer that I turned thirty-eight, life was again beginning to unravel. My then sixteen-year-old and I came out to each other. We had numerous conversations leading up to this, so neither one of us was overly shocked by the other's revelation.

A year later my second marriage was over. I was once again facing life as a single parent. This time choosing to live an openly authentic life as a proud gay woman. Except that I wasn't a woman at all.

In March 2017 the woman I was dating at the time asked me if I was trans. Completely taken aback, I immediately said "NO" but in my head my thoughts were screaming "I am totally trans!"

This was the first time I both realized and accepted that I was transgender.

Over four decades earlier I was assigned female at birth (AFAB) but that never fit. I never understood why it didn't bother me when people assumed that I was a little boy because I always had short hair and wore my brother's hand-me-downs as often as I could, or why I beamed inside every time I got to play the boy during make believe games with my best friend.

At that time it really didn't matter, I certainly wasn't going to transition. I was riddled with fear of the unknowns. What would that do to my kids? And what would it do to my identity?

Up until then, my entire life's purpose could be wrapped up in being a mom. If I'm not in fact a mom, what am I? Who am I? My whole life I've struggled with a lack of self-worth. How would I ever find the success I longed for if I exposed my true gender?

The more I tried to ignore the fact that I was transgender, the more I couldn't.

In August 2017 I started doing peer counselling with a non-binary trans masculine person. They helped me work through my issues **with being a mom and a man**. They encouraged me to seek out healthy positive single dads, work from home dads, and gay dads to model. This work changed my perspective immensely. I found amazing examples of fathers who are nurturers, hands on dads who I could really resonate with. I realized that I can be the parent I've always been while also having a fulfilling successful business.

I swayed back and forth for another year before I was finally able to admit to myself and my family that I wanted to start testosterone injections. During that time, I also had uncertainty about medically transitioning because there was this small part of me that wondered—hoped—if maybe I just needed to work through my trauma of being sexually abused as a child and that would "fix" me.

I wanted nothing more than to pack up all of my issues and separate them into two boxes, a "because I'm trans" box and a "because I was sexually abused" box. Unfortunately, most of my issues couldn't fit in either box and were likely a tangled knot of both.

I made the decision to take testosterone like I make every other choice in my life, I trusted my intuition. Although my life has been full of twists and turns, I've yet to regret any decisions I've made relying on my intuition.

So here I am, nearly forty-four years old, almost twenty years after coming out the first time, finally living my truth.

I am a transgender life coach. Authenticity and self-acceptance are the foundations of my career. I spend my days empowering others to find, accept, acknowledge, and live their most authentic lives whether that fits in a neat little societally accepted box or not. Typically for my clients, their truest selves don't even know what the word "box" means!

Living my truth, being able to live my life authentically, out loud and proud, provides the opportunity for other trans folks and even parents of trans kids to see that not only is it okay to be transgender, it's also something to celebrate.

We see examples everyday of cisgender heterosexual people

who have successful careers, relationships, families, and community.

When I was coming out, I had access to none of that, **so I became my own example**.

I am living proof that being trans does not have to be a deterrent from living and celebrating a wildly fulfilled life and career as an LGBTQ+ person.

Expressing my truth came with some rejection and loss but everything I've gained has been unimaginably wonderful and worth it.

As Marianne Williamson said, "For every person who might reject you if you live your truth, there are ten others who will embrace you and welcome you home."

So I ask you, what is your truth?

How can you use it to fuel a life and career you can love and fully live in?

Are you ready to live as your whole self and find financial success through the people who will embrace you and welcome you home?

If so, this book is the launching pad you've been waiting for.

We're happy to have you with us.

DEAN RASMUSSEN

Dean (he/they) is a transgender man rebelling against the binary every chance they can. He and his partner Julie are parents to eight remarkably unique humans, two of which are also trans. With a coming out story spanning nearly twenty years, a few sexualities, and more than one gender, Dean has finally discovered what it means to live their most authentic life and spends his days teaching others how to do the same. Dean is a Life Coach whose passions are empowering the LGBTQ2S community, especially later in life transgender folks, parenting, and personal growth. In many ways they're just your everyday guy, in other ways, he is quite the anomaly!

Website: everydayanomalycoaching.ca

2

A BRIEF FIELD GUIDE TO QUEER STORYTELLING

Trauma is the currency of the LGBTQ+ business space. We wheel and deal in devastation and lived experience, rehashing pain in the name of relatability. Some of us never launch our offers or retract them altogether for fear of having to out ourselves or face the trauma we fear lies ahead. Whether it's done consciously or not, many of us feel the need to expose one scar after the other in order to make our clients, customers, and peers feel more at ease around us. After all, the more we share, the more folks will see themselves in us, right?

My question for you is: At what cost? If you are an LGBTQ+ human choosing to cater your work to the community, what emotional taxes are you paying as a result of your decision to lay it all out?

What boundaries have you set in place for yourself? And how are you managing the psychological labor that goes into putting those puzzle pieces together for your audience to ingest?

Dig in.

When did you learn the need to share so much of your heaviness? When did the cost of burnout and daily psychological labor become a job requirement for you? Did you truly leave your 9-5 to trade one form of burnout for another?

Many of my own relationships early on in my entrepreneurial journey were rooted in trauma bonding. Networking felt like a breeze because, if we're honest, it wasn't networking. It was an exchange of painful experiences. Although those connections led to incredible things, I found myself depleted at the end of each workday.

If you've been there and you're now thinking about how many times you've done the same, there's no shame. Whether you choose to work with a copywriter or not, there are plenty of ways to avoid self-harm in your business's storytelling. Let's walk through some of the basics.

The roadmap to "feel good" queer storytelling.

Just in case no one has ever told you: *Your business doesn't HAVE to be about your queerness.* You can make products, offer services, and conduct a whole ass operation that caters to the queer community without any specific storytelling about your own identity or sexuality.

However, if you choose to carry the torch and be out in your business, here are my six top tips for sorting through how to deliver impactful storytelling, while respecting your personal boundaries:

Get your ass into therapy

I know it can be expensive and it's not always accessible to everyone, but if you have the ability to, get professional support. Being a part of this community is heavy—working within this community can be heavier. Having confidential support along the way can make all the difference in your personal life and within your business.

Often, I find that folks can identify what feels good to share professionally through therapy alone. For many of us, including myself, therapy was the first place we came out. Imagine the impact of that safe container for your professional efforts. Think of it as a filter through which you can sift out trauma you don't want expressed within your business.

Identify who you are talking to (know your audience)

I know you know this rule. It's one of the fundamentals of any form of marketing but here's why it makes a difference in queer content writing:

- When identifying your LGBTQ+ audience, you need to go beyond binary thinking. Standard language isn't going to fly here so we need to dig a little deeper. When you say you serve "queer women" or "queer men," what does that actually mean? **Be intentional with your language.**
- How can you address your clients' needs without exploiting their trauma? You might think that telling your own story would make them feel safe and seen, but what if it triggers them instead? By taking the time to know your audience, you can intentionally deliver marketing that is trauma-aware while avoiding taking the burden of responsibility for others' triggers.
- What does your relationship to the audience look like? Are you a thought leader, space holder, or an old-fashion service provider? This will dictate your tone and how you show up for your people.

For example: As a copywriting consultant, it's my job to deliver authoritative storytelling and let my audience know I'm here to either work with or for them to deliver impactful stories. It's much less personal and not all that much about my own experience as a queer person. In contrast, a coming-out coach may want to share a TON about their history because the folks coming to them want to know they'll be working with someone who has been in their shoes, savvy?

Discern what feels good, safe, and relevant to share

This is where most of us get stuck. For this portion of the work, I like to go old school with pen and paper, but a mental list will do just fine.

Divide your paper into two columns. Above the first column, write "public knowledge" and under the second column, write "what's scary/harmful to share."

Spend some time diving in on this. You can start with things you've already posted about or shared with your audience. If anything feels harmful or scary, let it be a boundary in the future. You don't need to go there anymore.

From there, you can either brainstorm through your history or possibly look at what others have shared in their marketing and ask yourself, "Would I want to share this about myself?" By the time the exercise is over, you should have an idea of your personal boundaries.

When in doubt, skip everything that isn't directly addressing your clients'/customers' needs and how you can solve them. As business owners and leaders, it is our job to teach from a place of lessons learned versus from a place of hurt/woundedness. We aren't doing anyone any favors if the painful stories never end in a teachable moment. I don't mean to say that everything *must* be a teachable moment. I simply mean that if it wasn't, then it's maybe not worth mentioning to your audience.

Develop a lexicon

A lexicon is an extension of the exercise above. In short, it's a personalized written guide to your language boundaries as a business owner.

Some of the most successful copy projects I've worked on have been because the business owner was firm on their lexicon.

Whether it simply means throwing in a "y'all" or a "buddy" here and there, developing this vocabulary will not only help contractors or consultants like me, but will also ensure your customers have a consistent experience of your tone in all facets of your business.

It may seem like a simple list of words wouldn't make all that much of a difference. But few people take the time to think through how they describe what they do, what words encapsulate those services best and how to deliver the persona they are looking to achieve. As a result, there can be harm done, miscommunications, and fogginess around what the business actually does or how they do it.

Jargon can only get you so far; people are smart and LGBTQ+ consumers are even smarter. Your lexicon should define the words that best speak to your brand's personality, honor your business boundaries, and inform on what language is unacceptable to use.

How to omit

Storytelling is an intimate experience which often means we get caught up in our own heads. If we're blindly sharing, we may unintentionally burn ourselves out and, again, trigger the trauma of our readers.

People want to feel safe with you, yes. Authority and effective storytelling are crucial, sure. But, if you would rather take the trauma-informed route and whittle down the nitty gritty details, here's an example of how to do so.

- Tell someone else's story (often done through testimonials)
- Remove the history from your copy

For context, let's walk through copy on a social post WITH personal storytelling:

"Do you remember your first '*ah-ha!*' moment?

The first time you ever encountered an openly LGBTQ+ person in the wild? Just an everyday human, passing by on the street, ordering a coffee, or walking their dog.

For me, it was my manager at a steakhouse that I worked for post-college. Growing up in Oklahoma, it never quite felt safe to admit my sexuality, even to myself, let alone to let it show externally.

And yet there she was.

Openly queer, wife, baby on the way... living as confidently as can be.

Working with her, I heard countless conversations about day-to-day life—how excited she and her partner were to pick out nursery room items, how she and her wife had met, career goals, etc.

These conversations may have seemed insignificant to everyone else, but to me, they were the evidence I didn't know I had been looking for. I realized if she could be herself, if she could live a full and authentic life... so could I.

So, I came out.

Her visibility was the catalyst to an entirely new life for me. I can only hope that one day someone else will look to me as their example. An inspiration to be visible.

Let's hear your "*ah-ha!*" moment in the comments below!"

Here is that same social post with the personal aspects of the story removed:

"Do you remember your first '*ah-ha!*' moment?

The first time you ever encountered an openly LGBTQ+ person in the wild? Just an everyday human, passing by on the street, ordering a coffee, or walking their dog.

For many LGBTQ+ folk, especially for those who grew up in religion or small towns, these moments come much later in life.

Even if there's an inkling of queerness, it never seems like a reality in early life because living proof is scarce.

How many years of your life did you spend denying your authentic self? At what age did you realize being openly queer was even an option? Who unknowingly granted you a permission slip to be visible?

Share with me in the comments below!"

Both social posts deliver the same impact. Both allow the audience to relate to the queer experience and relive a positive experience within their life. The only difference? One of them required less energy from the author than the other.

Whether utilizing facts, statistics, or testimonials, there are a billion ways to avoid sprinkling in information from your personal background. You can absolutely deliver impactful storytelling, get your point across, AND make your audience feel seen using the tactics above.

RECOGNIZE the fluidity of your narrative

Your business is a living and breathing entity. It will forever be evolving, growing, shrinking; constantly in a state of metamorphosis. You may find yourself in cycles of certainty and questioning.

Stay grounded and know that you are totally in control of the narrative. You choose how to present your business from day to day. You ARE the business. **Your story will be as fluid as you are.**

WHETHER YOU CHOOSE to divulge your queerness in your storytelling, or simply use it as inspiration to guide your copywriting, your presence in the business space is a form of activism in itself. You can conserve your trauma dollars wherever you see fit because your sheer visibility in this space paves the way for others after you to be visible as well. Through queer storytelling, we maintain our shared narrative, the only history book we've ever had.

BRAIDYN BROWNING

Braidyn Browning (They/Them) is a Content and Copywriting Consultant for LGBTQ+ owned and allied businesses. Growing up in a small town in Oklahoma, Braidyn lived within books and stories that felt more like "home" than the environment around them. Once Braidyn entered the entrepreneurial space, they realized the power of queer storytelling and how sheer visibility could create a home for others too. Braidyn now spends their days traveling the United States with their two dogs in a self-converted van and helps business owners deliver impactful and trauma-informed storytelling for LGBTQ+ folks.

Website: itsbraidyn.com
Instagram: @itsbraidyn

3

INTENTIONAL EMPATHY

As we humans continue to evolve in the digital age with more access than ever to the unique experiences of people all over the world, emotional awareness has become more and more of an essential ingredient in nearly every sector of life, including business. Whether we work for a non-profit or a billion-dollar corporation, our society is beginning to recognize the value of integrating good mental health practices in any environment. Recent global initiatives such as the Me Too movement and Black Lives Matter have also raised our awareness to the major impact that things like trauma, discrimination, and other unique experiences have on those around us. Companies can no longer expect to manage employees or conduct business without taking emotional awareness into account. In this chapter I will introduce the tool of Intentional Empathy and demonstrate how the age of emotional awareness can, not only make us more successful, but improve our collective quality of life in a very meaningful way.

The concept of Intentional Empathy first got my attention when I was working with a mental health crisis intervention team stationed in the Dallas County Jail (aka the Lew Sterrett Justice

Center). If you aren't familiar, the Dallas County Jail has about 6,000 inmates booked in at any given moment and it is considered the second largest mental health facility in the state of Texas.

My job was to interview inmates regarding their mental health, offer some brief therapeutic interventions, and get them connected to resources and treatment that might prevent future clashes with law enforcement.

I knew when I accepted the position that it was going to be a challenging job. I was not prepared, however, for how difficult it was going to be for me to offer some of my clients the unconditional empathy that I am used to giving in my role as a therapist.

Initially, my main challenge was when male inmates would masturbate in the visitation booth while I was trying to do therapy with them. I quickly learned how to express firm boundaries while also recognizing that their sexually inappropriate behavior did not mean they were not worth my time and compassion.

I had hoped that would be the most difficult challenge I'd face but I was very, very wrong.

A few months into my time working at the jail, I was assigned to meet with an inmate who was arrested for the alleged sexual assault of a minor. Not only that, but according to his record, he had previously been convicted of that same crime *twice* before and had spent a significant amount of time in prison for it. I instantly felt my heart sink.

In my career as a therapist, I have worked with numerous victims of childhood sexual assault. I myself was a victim of sexual assault when I was only eight years old. As you can imagine, someone convicted of this type of crime was the *last person* in the world that I wanted to empathize with.

For the purposes of this chapter, let's call him Joe. Although I could have referred Joe to a colleague, I decided I wanted to challenge myself. Empathy is typically very second nature to me but in this case, I knew it would take intense effort. I got to work doing what I now refer to as *Intentional Empathy*.

My process of constructing Intentional Empathy was crude at first. It pulled from different things I had learned while getting my

Master's in counseling, while training for crisis intervention, and from my own personal experiences. The basic concept is that when someone does something that you can't understand or don't agree with, you have to start with some non-judgmental investigation to figure out their possible reasons.

When you're trying to engage in civil conversation with someone, you can't just throw your hands up and say "you're crazy! There's no talking sense to you!" That would obviously end the productive conversation immediately. Philosophy on human behaviors says that we humans don't do things for no reason at all. We have reasons, we have explanations, we have learned instincts, we have back stories. When someone acts in a way I don't relate to, I know that means I need to go into "detective mode" and start gathering as many clues as I can to understand their reasons and motivations.

Intentional Empathy has grown and evolved over the years with the help of my amazing business partner and best friend, Josh Miller (his chapter is up next in this book). Although I didn't have all the terms yet, this was the framework that I used as I sat in my office outside the Dallas County Jail preparing to offer help to a convicted child rapist.

In its most basic form, Intentional Empathy can be boiled down to this simple Empathy Equation:

Identity + Experience + Circumstance = Feelings & Behaviors

To put it into the form of a statement, "Based on who you are, what you've been through, and what's been going on lately, the way that you are feeling and behaving is understandable."

Sounds pretty basic, right? As I started using this framework to prepare for my meeting with Joe, I knew I was going to need more information to work with. Who was he? Where was he from? What had his life been like? What was he likely feeling right now? I started doing research. Using the compiled information, I had from public court records and from our prior interactions with him, I found out as much as I could about him.

Joe was Black and had grown up in the poorest area of Dallas. He never finished high school and was raised by one parent. He'd been diagnosed with several different mental illnesses in the past, but as far as I knew, he'd never received any treatment. Additionally, I pulled from the things I knew about perpetrators of sexual violence and inmates who have been incarcerated for this type of crime.

I created a picture in my mind of Joe, adding as much detail as I could. The information I knew so far told me he'd had a hard life. Being a person of color in the south, from low socioeconomic status, with little education, and having untreated mental illness meant he had to navigate life with some very significant disadvantages.

Statistics indicate that people who perpetrate sexual violence on others are almost always victims of sexual assault first, most often in childhood. The violation or disregard of consent early in life can lead some to misunderstand the importance of getting consent from others. This meant that Joe had likely been a victim of sexual assault before he was even out of childhood. I also knew that inmates who are incarcerated for these types of crimes are treated terribly in prison, often being routinely abused and deprived of their basic needs.

My empathy for Joe was growing but I knew I still had to set aside my judgment to the best of my ability. I forced myself to look past the inexcusable behaviors that had landed him in jail, and tried to focus on all the pain, the trauma, and the neglect that had contributed to his worldview and his choices. I imagined seeing life through his eyes, feeling the overwhelming shame, hurt, confusion, and anger he must have experienced.

By the time I walked into that visitation booth, my disgust with his actions was still present but I did not hate him. I was able to treat him with dignity and compassion because I knew that he was not just an inflictor of pain, but a recipient. He responded with shocked gratitude and vulnerability, clearly not accustomed to being treated like a human being. His receptiveness and my own genuine desire to help him told me that I had discovered something very important.

Although you may not have to interview convicted child molesters in your field of work, I can safely assume that you have to interact with people you don't like from time to time. Your success personally and professionally depends on your ability to be diplomatic and respectful no matter how much you dislike or disagree with someone. Some industries require professionals to have conversations about sensitive topics that take a delicate approach.

You probably know what it feels like to be afraid that you will betray your disdain for someone else's opinions or choices and miss out on an opportunity. Additionally, in order for the LGBTQ+ population to continue gaining respect and equality, we have to be able to have hard conversations with people in an empathetic way.

Prior to working in mental health, I had several jobs in customer service and I experienced my share of uncomfortable confrontations. I've had disagreements in my personal and professional life that made me afraid that if I looked at things from my opponent's perspective, it would be too painful, I would feel dishonest, or it would open me up to compromising my values. If you can relate to that inner conflict, using Intentional Empathy might bring you some much-needed relief and empowerment.

Intentional Empathy is most easily used in situations where you know a lot about the person you're trying to empathize with or have the time to ask them questions. We don't always have that luxury, though. Working with someone who you don't know much about doesn't mean that Intentional Empathy is going to be impossible; it just means you will need to use your imagination and be willing to offer them the benefit of the doubt.

Let's use a hypothetical scenario to picture this. Imagine that you are an entrepreneur who is working to get your company off the ground, and you need each of your employees to do their jobs well so that you can keep paying everyone. One of your employees, Janet, has been calling in "sick" repeatedly lately. Her taking so many personal days causes you to scramble to get her work covered by her peers even though everyone else has a full workload already. Additionally, when Janet does make it to work, she appears irritated, distracted, and doesn't seem to acknowledge how hard her team has been working to accommodate for her absences. If you're using Intentional Empathy, you know that Janet must have reasons for her feelings and behaviors. Privacy agreements, however, dictate that you can't force Janet to explain her situation to you. What do you do?

As the business owner, you know that if Janet continues on this path, she is going to lose her job. You also recognize that the conversation you need to have with her is going to be difficult for both of you and won't go well if you aren't being empathetic. It's time to go into investigation mode and start thinking of some of the possible reasons why Janet may be acting this way. In the Empathy Equation words, you want to consider how her identity, experiences, and circumstances might explain her feelings and behaviors.

Is she experiencing health issues that have required her to go to doctors repeatedly lately? Is she struggling to find childcare that she can afford? Is she dealing with stressful family issues? Is she experiencing depression, anxiety, grief, or some other mental health concern? Is she being harassed by someone at work and trying to avoid them? There are a million possible reasons for her behavior that could legitimately explain her need to be out of work and irritability when she does make it into the office. What about past experiences that might be playing into the situation? Is it possible she has never worked in a job like this before and doesn't understand the problem with her behavior? Was she raised in a household where embarrassment was expressed through irritability or defensiveness? Has she been shamed or fired by employers in the past? There are a multitude of possible contributing factors that could make her behavior understandable, even if it's still problematic.

If you've intentionally thought about these possibilities, it doesn't matter that you don't know which of them is actually the case for Janet. Simply by imagining plausible and understandable explanations, you likely have overcome a lot of the irritation that you felt when you were only looking at her problematic behaviors but not considering her reasons.

When Janet comes to your office to meet with you, your tone and demeanor are likely to convey respect rather than disdain. You will be more open to hearing her explanation (if she chooses to give it) and you will be less inclined to be unnecessarily harsh. Although you will still need to hold her accountable for her missed work, you can do it in a way that makes her feel valued.

Janet is likely to leave the meeting feeling understood and motivated to prove to you that your willingness to give her the benefit of the doubt was justified. Not only did Intentional Empathy spare you from a conflict and potentially having to replace an employee, but it also established a rapport that made Janet (and other employees who were watching) more inclined to work hard for you. It showed that emotional intelligence is not just something you talk about, but something you put into practice.

If you want to implement Intentional Empathy in your work and personal life, the good news is that it's not a complicated process. The bad news is that you will have to do the uncomfortable work of challenging your biases and judgements. The steps of Intentional Empathy are the following:

1. **Be Curious.** Observe your reactions to others from a non-judgmental standpoint. If you feel uncomfortable, angry, or anxious while interacting with someone, don't ignore it. Listen to what your feelings are telling you and be open to investigating and challenging your biases.

2. **Suspend Judgment.** If you don't agree with someone's opinions or choices, you will need to "press pause" on your disagreement temporarily while you try to understand why someone would believe what they

believe. Remember: You don't have to agree to empathize.

3. **Gather Information.** Find out as much as you can about the person you're empathizing with. Ask questions and listen. Investigate the context they are living in and listen to others who have had similar experiences.

4. **Communicate Empathy.** You've cultivated empathy internally but now you need to say it out loud if it's going to make a real difference. Validation ("your feelings and experiences matter") and normalization ("you're not alone in this") are great starting points.

5. **Proceed With Openness.** Now that you've demonstrated that you respect the other person despite your differences, speak your own opinions with a tone of humility and willingness to learn something new.

WHETHER YOU'RE TALKING to an unhappy customer at work or having a debate with a family member about politics, implementing Intentional Empathy will decrease the likelihood of unnecessary conflict and increase the probability that you will have a productive conversation. By humanizing one another and by understanding why others may have different views, we gain a unique ability to demonstrate that we are listening, caring, and offering the same compassion to others that we would like to receive.

Many of us in the LGBTQ+ community know what it feels like to interact with someone who isn't practicing Intentional Empathy. Like me, you may have been deeply hurt by things that others have said from a place of ignorance or judgement. Fortunately, we also each know the incredible power of having someone choose to offer us empathy. Rather than continuing the cycle of harm and alienation that seems to be the status quo, we have the incredible opportunity to make the world a better place by modeling Intentional Empathy.

THE EMPATHY PARADIGM is a consulting business focused on teaching empathy skills to employers, educators, politicians, religious leaders, and more. Our goal is to promote positive change by creating a respectful platform for dialogue where difficult topics can be addressed.

ANNA MILLER

Anna Miller (she/her) is a Licensed Professional Counselor and the co-founder of The Empathy Paradigm, a mental health consulting business. As a therapist she works with clients dealing with issues including trauma, identity exploration, religious abuse, relationship issues, and more. She's a proud member of the LGBTQ+ community and is passionate about raising awareness, educating, and promoting empathy for those in our world who don't yet have the representation and equality they deserve.

Website: www.empathyparadigm.com
Instagram: https://instagram.com/empathyparadigm
Email: Theempathyparadigm@gmail.com

4

EMPATHIC LEADERSHIP

Expanding back as far as the 1940s, our cultural discourse has been slowly transitioning away from emotional ignorance and exclusion, into spaces of awareness and exploration. Ongoing civil rights efforts, specifically in the year 2020, have forced an operational evolution with empathy as the new *modus operandi* of a healthy and successful workplace. Anna Miller, co-founder of the Empathy Paradigm and author of the previous chapter, discussed Intentional Empathy and the formulaic breakdown used to conceptualize and understand ourselves and others. In this chapter, we'll look at how our understanding and implementation of Intentional Empathy can create an effective and empathic leader.

I was lucky enough to grow up in a middle-class home with both of my parents who loved me, but the unfortunate truth of a cis-heteronormative culture is that I've always been "othered." Long before I had the language to describe the feeling, I knew that I was different and that different was bad. I was labeled "boy," and I was expected to play and think like a boy despite my interests also lying elsewhere. I had to be a hyper-masculine barbarian for Halloween while my sister got to be Minnie Mouse. I had to play with the incredibly homoerotic G.I. Joes while my sister got to dress up her problematically thin Barbies in the most beautiful and colorful clothing. Aberrant behavior and interests were quickly corrected, forcing a recognition that parts of what made me uniquely me were unacceptable. If I wanted people to be happy, I would need to be what they wanted me to be.

Elementary school reinforced this indoctrination.

Now, I don't know if you know this, but kids are horrible. They're mean, especially in packs. Anything different about a student is isolated and amplified for all to see and make fun of, and I was an easy target. I was already hyper aware of the parts of me that made me different, and I was terrified that my class-mates would look too closely and see those flaws and imperfec-tions. I was terrified that my classmates would see me. So, instead, I became a chameleon of sorts. I learned how to manipulate the image that others saw when they looked at me by adjusting my personality and identity to their expectations.

"You know the new song on the radio? Me too."
"You've beaten that video game? I did it a year ago."
"You like basketball? Watch me hit this 3."
"You like kids that are polite? Yes, ma'am."

MANY OF US in the LGBTQIA+ community have similar stories, plus or minus some trauma. The indoctrination of compulsory heteronormativity and cisgenderism, combined with systemic oppression, create an inherent belief that we are flawed, and that we must make up for that deficiency through compliance with the respective social contracts of our environment.

Boys are tough, not tender. Girls are feminine and sexy. Nerds are curious, and jocks are dumb. Farmers are country bumpkins. I was expected to be a cisgendered straight male, and I was expected to meet the standards for a cisgendered straight male.

"Vulnerability? Never heard of her."

"Crying? You mean eye sweat."
"Provider of the household!"
"Spiritual leader?"
"Pressure and stress, and no outlets because therapy is for
pussies!"

It took years of deconstructing my identity and ideologies to find the well-hidden and disguised parts of me that truly belonged to me. I had to start opening lockboxes that had rusted shut and knock down walls with layers upon layers of bricks from years of reinforcement. I had to closely examine the things I was taught to look away from and embrace the discomfort I was taught to fear. Through vulnerability, curiosity, and intentionality, I was able to create the person I wanted to be and find freedom in the process. If that sounds familiar to you, it's because vulnerability and curiosity are key concepts of Intentional Empathy.

When we think back to what we've learned about Intentional Empathy, who comes to mind as someone that we should show empathy to? Is it Janet from the last chapter? A person experiencing homelessness or a member of another marginalized population? **Did you think of yourself?** Most likely not.

It sounds counter-intuitive since empathy is generally understood to be unilateral (meaning it only extends one way); however, Intentional Empathy is bilateral, impacting the person receiving it **and** the one giving it. When we exercise vulnerability and curiosity in our conceptualization of others, we normalize interrupting the patterns of assumptions and judgments that influence how we view ourselves.

I came out as gay in 2016, but I didn't come out as gender fluid until 2019. Those three years were spent reconciling my understanding of gender with what I was taught about gender, and what gender means for me. I hadn't been exposed to any gender diverse representation growing up, and my religion had weaponized their scriptures to instill transphobia and a disdain for non-binary gender expression. I couldn't conceptualize gender diversity on my own, so I had to educate myself with the help of friends at every opportunity.

It was embarrassing and uncomfortable at times, but I was recognizing my implicit biases and began to actively deconstruct and then work against them. I consumed literature, I went to drag shows, I asked questions, and I listened intently. I wanted to understand them, and I was fortunate enough to have friends that wanted to teach.

One friend in particular, a local drag performer, swapped stories with me on a few different occasions. We'd see each other at house parties or at the bar while they were performing, but we always found time to have intentional conversations. I didn't understand their art, but I wanted to be supportive. I started asking questions about their introduction to drag and more details about their drag persona. I asked about their pronouns and about their understanding of the nuanced gender identity and expression labels. They were vulnerable and introspective, taking time to think through their answers. It was obvious they had thought about these topics in-depth before.

Our conversations about gender were a mirror that reflected many of the thoughts and feelings I had when I was younger. As I stared into my reflection, I saw the person I had locked away take shape. The words my friend was using to describe their journey were the keys I needed to unlock that part of my identity. Exercising Intentional Empathy in order to understand my gender diverse friends helped me reach a deeper understanding of myself and identify some of my indoctrinated beliefs. Once identified, I chose to address them. **That is the basis of Empathic Leadership.**

If Intentional Empathy can be described as the process of understanding ourselves and others, then Empathic Leadership is using that understanding to change the way we connect to ourselves and others. Like the Penrose Stair, both exist independently but rely on the other to exist. You cannot climb up the staircase of Empathic Leadership without also climbing down the staircase of Intentional Empathy. The key to understanding which direction you're climbing is whether or not a lasting change takes place.

Curiosity and vulnerability on their own are change agents. When we're curious, we're creating space for a change in understanding. When we're vulnerable, we're creating space for a change in connection. Therefore, Intentional Empathy, utilizing both curiosity and vulnerability to build understanding, creates the space for change, which, in and of itself, is a change. It is an interruption of patterns of assumptions and judgments. We move into Empathic Leadership when we allow that interruption to create lasting change, and we create lasting change through ongoing Intentional Empathy.

I exercised Intentional Empathy with my friend, and in doing so, I interrupted the perpetuation of the same mindsets and cycles of behavior that forced me to lock away my gender curiosity and sexual expressions when I was young. The conversations made me uncomfortable because I had to confront hard truths about myself and my childhood. I could have turned away from the discomfort and let the interruption lapse. Instead, I pressed in. I found other topics that made me uncomfortable and other facets of human existence that I didn't understand or "agree" with. I continued asking hard questions and getting hard answers, and, as a result, I continued interrupting my assumptions and judgments.

The new spaces created by the interruption allowed new ways of thinking and behaving to grow and take form. The new ways now occupied those spaces, and there was nowhere left for the old assumptions and judgements to remain. My intentionality in the interruptions led me to new relationships, new opportunities, and new understandings of myself.

For me, the commitment to self-reflection and awareness is one of the hardest parts of Empathic Leadership. As a result of growing up in a high-control faith system, I was taught that my beliefs were not only true, but that they had divine backing. Doubting my beliefs, or the ones that taught them, resulted in damnation.

As a child, I didn't know how to separate and challenge the

individual components of my worldview, and that led to me understanding what I was taught to believe about any given topic was undeniably true. Anytime I began peeling away the layers of indoctrination, I would catch glimpses of what was waiting within and quickly end the exercise.

Truthfully, I knew that I had things hidden in there that I didn't want to face, which I think is true for many of us. When we are confronted by the things that we could change, we must decide if we truly want to change them - and that decision point is scary as Hell.

What would it mean to admit that there are parts of myself that I should change? What does it mean if I don't want to change those parts? Through Intentional Empathy, I wrestled with those questions and interrupted the cycle.

"What cycles of mine need to be interrupted?"
"What layers do I need to peel back?"
"What is upholding my established worldviews and ideologies?"

It's important to note that as we continue to evolve and change as people, so will our answers to these questions. As humans, we are constantly absorbing new ideas and adjusting our beliefs to reconcile the new information and how we react to it. Consequently, we cannot become complacent in our commitment to self-reflection and intentional examination of what we find.

Use the above questions as a starting point, and then add to them. Explore them, change them, and develop them further. Meditate on them and seek out information in a medium you enjoy in books, podcasts, blogs, social media conversations, therapy, or other. Take a course on allyship development or multicultural competencies. Whatever process works best for you, dedicate yourself entirely to it and be consistent. Remember, consistent interruption is the key to lasting change, and lasting change through vulnerability and curiosity is the crux of Empathic Leadership.

I personally have a goal journal where I write the question I want answered at the top, and then list the steps I'm going to take to get the answer. I always leave room for extra steps since I'm never sure how my journey to answering the question will change as I move and learn, but my steps always include "personal research" and "hard conversations" with room to expand on both.

One of my clients created a similar journal as she began her coming out journey as a leader in a faith community. The big question she wanted answered was, "Am I good?" Overwhelming, right? She also thought so and found it difficult to start her process. Asking herself that question meant taking a deep dive into her core beliefs and why she believed them, and that was uncomfortable. Similar to my religious upbringing, she was trained to believe that discomfort (one of the building blocks of curiosity and vulnerability) was ungodly. That indoctrination would need to be interrupted before her question could be answered, so I had her draw a line across the page. Under the line and with room to edit, I had her write smaller questions that would create smaller interruptions:

What does she believe about her sexuality?
Is it the same as what she was taught to believe?
Why does she believe it?
How do her beliefs shape her behaviors and thoughts?

UNDER EACH OF the smaller questions, I had her draw another line. From there, she wrote the steps she could take to find answers to her questions. Keep in mind that the point wasn't to find the exact right answer, but to ask the questions and search for an answer. By doing so, she interrupted her trained aversion to discomfort and uncertainty, and created the spaces to grow.

As she wrestled with the answers she found, she created the answer to her original question. Not only did she have her answer, but she understood why that was her answer. Yes, she was good, and it was through the consistent interruption of her indoctrinated beliefs and thoughts that helped her reach that conclusion. That became her foundation for coming out, and her ongoing journey now informs the way she teaches and leads in her faith community. Because she wrestled with whether or not she is good, she can empathize with others that ask the same question about her.

This work is difficult, but you aren't alone. The Empathy Paradigm is a consulting business specializing in teaching Intentional Empathy and Empathic Leadership. Our vision is to teach employers, educators, politicians, religious leaders, and more how to use empathy with the goal of interrupting personal and systemic discrimination. If we, together, can create a community, a workplace, a friend group, a relationship, or a single individual that builds a worldview on Empathic Leadership, then we can begin to see real change.

JOSH MILLER

Josh Miller, pronouns he/they, is a Mental Health Consultant based in Texas and the co-founder of The Empathy Paradigm, a full-service mental health consulting company specializing in creating trauma-informed and DEI-conscious spaces. His specialties include coming out coaching and allyship development, and he works to empower all individuals to explore and confidently express their identity and beliefs through advocacy for equality, representation, and inclusion.

Website: EmpathyParadigm.com
Instagram: @Josh_Dangit_tEP and @EmpathyParadigm

5

FROM BURN OUT TO GLOW UP

"The most disrespected person in America is the
black woman.
The most unprotected person in America is the
black woman.
The most neglected person in America is the black
woman."
- *from a speech Malcolm X gave May 22, 1962, in Los
Angeles*

Black women grow up learning from the world that we have to be twice as good to get half as far in life. We've become a beacon of nurturing for everyone else except ourselves and as a result, our light has dimmed. The pandemic put a spotlight on burnout and mental illness with much needed conversation around how we overwork employees in America. We are all burned out and desperately want to find a new normal.

We must begin with acknowledging and understanding how Black women have carried depression and burnout in our being as a result of racism for centuries. The oppression, abuse, and trauma against Black bodies, women especially, have led us to believe that burnout and depression are personal failures we should be ashamed of. Both racism and gender discrimination have profound impacts on the well-being of Black women. Despite the fact that Black women earned 66 percent of bachelor's degrees, 71 percent of master's degrees, and 65 percent of all doctorate degrees they still earn 38 percent less money than white men and 21 percent less money than white women.[1] Black women have always found a way to make a way out of no way but our bodies suffer (Lean In n.d.).[2] Our mental and emotional health suffers.

I suffered in silence. A high functioning, single mom, business professional who was active in the community and also severely depressed and burned out. I knew I was depressed but didn't realize how deeply. I just thought I was failing—at everything. I felt so alone.

I understand, now, I am not alone. I understand I wasn't failing; I just felt the trauma of generations of racism and patriarchy. I understand now that embracing my Blackness, my womanhood, my queerness, has been key to my healing and finding my purpose.

We all are vulnerable to depression and anxiety and the resulting burnout. We are all experiencing the same systems of oppression; however, we all have different outcomes, especially for those Black and queer in Madison, Wisconsin—the worst state for Black Americans.[3]

In my darkest moments of burnout, I found ways to reignite the light inside me to find my way back to myself so I can continue to carry the light for others. My healing called for me to observe how my pain was a mirror to what parts of me were most [4]broken and burned out. I was sick and tired of being sick and tired, and I know you are too!

Even if you feel all hope is gone, as long as you are breathing, your story goes on. This chapter is a healing space for you. Especially my Black sisters: I see you; I feel you, and there's brilliant infinite light inside you. Don't let the world dim your light; be your own damn guru and shine bright!

Safer at home

In 2019, I hit a wall that broke me apart. I spent much of the year super depressed yet high functioning and literally high. Every moment I could spare was spent hidden in my room numbing myself.

I had the best intentions, but I was too busy to really take care of myself. I advised others on self-care, yet I slacked with practicing this for myself. I was organized and strategic with my decisions. I've been on my own for a while and I knew how to successfully take care of my own shit, but during this time, I struggled to even get out of bed most days.

The year began with an exciting change of pace in my career. I moved from being a branch manager at a bank to a branch manager at a credit union. It was fast paced and seemingly provided the opportunity to serve members of color in the community. I managed two branch locations and still participated in volunteer events and facilitated workshops, joined a board of a non-profit, recorded a season of my podcast, and mentored a couple of young ladies. I also dived deeper into my spiritual practice and shadow work.

I began taking small steps to manifest my dreams of creating a life coaching and spiritual practice. I committed to writing more and finally finishing my two novels in progress. I supported my daughter through a stressful sophomore year of college. I got my son through the sixth grade and his football season.

A plot twist hit mid-year: A broken engagement with a man left me devastated and reevaluating my whole life and my sexuality.

And not to mention fucking racism! It's so retraumatizing watching the nonstop news coverage of the brutality against Black bodies and the constant debates on the value our lives hold. I experienced racism with my son at his school, my daughter at her college, at work, and in the community. I witnessed it with others and on social media and TV: It was all inescapable and hopeless.

The lack of accountability for the human rights violations against Black Americans and the gaslighting of racism, pushed me over the edge. I was woke AF and exhausted AF.

Cue writers block then panic attacks.

My depression worsened and I began doing something rarely done for self-care: calling in sick. One morning post panic attack, Spirit urged me to call to make an appointment with a new therapist. I knew I needed help and didn't have the energy to help myself anymore. None of my tools and coping mechanisms were working anymore. I felt my back up battery deteriorating as each day passed.

I spent much of the year grieving the death of who I knew myself to be and the life I was living. I didn't realize then that I was birthing unconditional love and light for the parts of me that society had subconsciously programmed me to be ashamed of and hate.

What does burnout look like?

PHYSICAL SIGNS and symptoms of burnout can include feeling exhausted and drained, lowered immunity, frequent headaches and muscle pain, change in appetite and sleep habits.

Emotional signs and symptoms can include feeling helpless, trapped, defeated, detached and alone. Imposter syndrome often creeps in, and you may feel like you can't get anything right. You could lose motivation and suddenly have this sense of dissatisfaction. It can feel like everyone and everything gets on your nerves.

Behavioral signs and symptoms include isolation, procrastination, withdrawal, or using food, drugs, or alcohol to cope. It can also look like someone taking their frustrations out on others.

More noticeably, skipping work or coming in late or dropping the ball on your responsibilities can indicate your light is dimming.

Burnout gained a spotlight and study as a medical syndrome in 1974 when psychologist Herbert Freudenberger published an article called "Staff Burnout." It wasn't until 2019 that burnout became an official diagnosis.

Burnout was found to be a significant predictor of physical consequences like hypercholesterolemia, type 2 diabetes, coronary heart disease, musculoskeletal pain, changes in pain experiences, prolonged fatigue, headaches, gastrointestinal issues, and respiratory problems. The psychological effects were insomnia, depressive symptoms, and psychological ill-health symptoms.[5]

Depression is a mixtape of the deepest darkest emotions humans can experience. It can bring feelings of sadness, emptiness, hopelessness, worthlessness, and guilt often leading to fixating on past failures and mistakes. This leads to trouble maintaining focus and attention, sleep disturbances, appetite changes, slowed thinking, speaking and often movements, unexplained physical problems, and personality changes. It's not just sadness; you can experience angry outbursts, irritability, frustration, loss of interest and all pleasure in the things you normally loved. At its worst, depression can lead to suicide.

*DISCLAIMER - If you are in crisis or you think you may have an emergency, call your doctor or 911 immediately. If you're having suicidal thoughts, call 1-800-273-TALK (8255) to talk to a skilled, trained counselor at a crisis center in your area at any time (National Suicide Prevention Lifeline) or text 741741. If you are located outside the United States, call your local emergency line immediately. It is not a sign of weakness; it takes immense strength to be the one who finds courage to ask for help for yourself. In those moments remember others are truly there for you. It may feel like you are a burden, and you may not want others to see you at your lowest but we all have been there. Allow others to be there and hold space for you. You don't have to go through this alone.

Holding a mirror to myself

THE DEFINITIONS and classifications of mental health conditions are often created by cisgendered white individuals who set the tone for normalcy and abnormality in society. Can you spot the racism and sexism in mental health diagnoses?

The trauma that racism and systems of oppression play in mental illness, especially with LGBTQ and Black Americans, is often ignored. Also ignored is the same role racism plays in continuing to retraumatize, dehumanize, and exacerbate mental health issues. It's in both the big and small moments of racism that burn us out. The interdependence of how we interact with the world and how it affects our mental, physical, and emotional bodies is far too complex to classify medically without factoring in the effects of racism and sexism. Would any of these issues exist in so many of us if racism and sexism didn't inflict the harm it does?

While researching the different types of burnout, like activism burnout and caregiver burnout, I can't help but offer myself grace and hold space to rest. Thinking of all my ancestors who were labeled "lazy" and beaten, killed, fired, and stereotyped, even today, for exhibiting prolonged burnout as a side effect of being in constant survival mode from racism, sexism, and systematic oppression as a whole, gave me cause to pause.

Our worth as humans is measured by our productivity. We all struggle to separate ourselves from our jobs. We push, we fight, we write, we speak, we march, we create, we hustle and side hustle, and we keep pushing. Until one day… SNAP!

My snap wasn't loud or dramatic. Well, it was dramatic, but it was quiet. The social media news feeds were focused on stories about COVID-19 in the early spring of 2020. The world was scrambling to understand this outbreak and I was scrambling to get control of my mental health.

I knew that this time, my healing was about saving my own life. This bout of darkness was different: my light felt like it was gone. I knew if I didn't figure out what my spirit was screaming to me, I wouldn't make it to see 2021.

I had made plans to take my own life in late 2019. D-day was planned for years in the future, but the plans were in place. Often, I'd wake up sweaty in panic attack mode unable to peel myself off the floor. My happy button was broken. My morning drive provided beautiful scenery of the lake on either side of me. I was stuck in traffic on John Nolen often but missed so many sunrise and sunset views because I was fantasizing about driving my SUV into the lake. That was not a part of the plan and way more dramatic than I wanted to go out, so it never happened.

Life is a drama meant to really be lived, and I felt like a background character in my own story. It was time for a fucking plot twist. I decided to just live and write my own story. Be present with purpose, on purpose. If shit hits the fan and doesn't work out, oh well, I don't want to be alive anyway.

Practicing Being You 2.0

PLOT TWIST! I quit my job. I had a mortgage, student loans, one kid about to get braces, another about to get her wisdom teeth out. Of course, my SUV needed repairs too. I had grown-up responsibilities, yet I woke up one morning and decided to quit my job—without a new job lined up. I just needed liberation! By Friday of the next week, I was home in the middle of the afternoon creating my vision and mission outlines and future notes to self and plotting my next moves.

I had a plan when I quit my job. I didn't share it with many, but it was there. It was hard to explain because I decided to have faith and focus on finding my purpose through healing myself. I wanted to use what I learned to tell stories and create a business to help others heal but I didn't know how that would look. I had a mission with different visions, but I didn't tie myself to every detail or a specific outcome.

Healing is not linear or predictable nor does it have to make sense to anyone except the person seeking healing. I always dreamt of going to a monastery to study and meditate. Not for years or the remainder of my life—I have kids and a partner, and I like to twerk and do illegal things and have sex—but maybe six months every three years.

I want to help heal my community, so I know I must be *here*. This moment.

My identity is grounded in my Blackness, but my spirit is rooted in my Buddhahood and my mysticism. I decided to create an ashram at home. Study and meditate in the space I create and control. That's where we will begin.

Creating a space for you to study and meditate on the subject of you. Make this time with yourself a priority and commit to the exploration of your healing for six months to start with daily prac-tice and the exploration of different directions of growth.

Be your own damn guru

To begin, you'll need a journal. A ginormous one and some pretty pens, because being extra is absolutely called for here. First rule of this journal is to always keep it real with yourself. Second, commit to having the courage to explore what your version of healing, joy, and success can be. There is no right or wrong way and no perfect way. Third, commit to exploring and playing, not seeking answers or achieving a goal. As a matter of fact, let go of the idea of always needing to achieve a goal. Replace that with finding a mission your soul can carry out in this lifetime in a variety of ways. This journal will help you create visions for how it could manifest daily and give you space to dream. All change begins and ends with the words you think, speak, and write.

· · ·

1. Routine. Take a few weeks to observe and document your own routines. Start with your daily routine from waking up to falling asleep. Pay special attention to the actions and obligations that drain you or bring unwanted emotions and outcomes. Bonus points if you also document your routine thoughts and emotions. Ask yourself hard questions, challenge your own thoughts and beliefs. **Remember**, we can't often change the world around us, but we can change how we perceive it and react to it and allow it to affect us. Don't be afraid to adjust your actions if you find a part of your routine doesn't serve your highest good.

- Tip: Create a routine or ritual around journaling and spending this quality time with yourself.

2. WTF is wrong with me? Here is where I started. A four-page letter to myself detailing what I didn't like about myself and my life. I was brutal to myself, and it was beautiful. I read it out loud to myself in the mirror, naked, because why not add more torture, right? I ugly cried till snot ran down my face then I took a red Sharpie and wrote "I am divinely perfect" in big bold letters on each page. I burned the pages and started over and wrote an eight-page letter to myself with all the things that are right and unique about me despite the "wrong" things. I wrote down big dreams about the things that only I could bring to the world with my talents and uniqueness. This letter I keep and reread from time to time when I feel low and add to it as I grow. It was a liberating labor of love I recommend you try.

3. Self-exploration for liberation and light. I created journal prompts that allowed me to reexamine my perspective of myself and my life. I rewrote the story I was telling myself about what I was worthy of. My focus was three areas of personal evolution: mind, body, and soul. To get to the core of those areas I needed to understand some key things. The primary element is the social, political, and racial climate, currently and historically. What am I up against externally? Having that foundation fuels your why and

allows your dreams to exist outside of your individual desires. You develop a mission tied to something larger than yourself.

- Tip: This is a manifestation hack many folks miss. Make your desires and dreams be around things that serve your highest good and also the highest good of others and the universe will have your back.

A. WHO ARE YOU? Know yourself better than anyone else. Explore these aspects of yourself. Mind: Personality type, zodiac traits, numerology, strengths, weaknesses. Discover what brings you joy, what frustrates you. Are you an introvert or extrovert? Body: What is an optimal diet for you? Sleep pattern? How do you exercise and celebrate your body? Soul: What is your spiritual practice and why? How often do you meditate or sit alone with yourself? How do you nurture yourself and take care of your own needs? What other self-exploration questions could you come up with?

B. WHAT DO you want and why? Be selfish in how you love yourself so that love overflows and you can better love others unconditionally. When you're used to giving so much to others it can feel selfish to give to yourself first, but it is the highest honor to yourself. Do you desire fame, wealth, health, love? Can you examine the things you want and where that desire came from? Can you consider how obtaining the object of your desire will serve the highest good of yourself and others? How do these desires drive your actions or inaction? Why do you want these things anyway? Has media, commercialism, religion, or your community made you believe these things are important for you? Who benefits when you get what you want? Who is burdened? What do you stand to lose if you don't get what you want? The biggest question and one that will test you most: How can you remain committed to your mission even if the vision doesn't look or feel like you want?

C. <u>Note to self</u>. Here's another personal journal hack that helps me. After I observed myself, my routines, I examined how my thoughts and actions were serving my highest good. The aspects of my routine that I observed that no longer served me had to be replaced with new things. Those items become a note to self. These are literal sticky notes around my house with reminders of triggers to watch for, things to stop doing, or begin to practice doing. Affirmations, mantras, song lyrics or movie quotes, make your notes to self your love letters to yourself. Get creative with how you hold yourself accountable, practice new habits and encourage yourself until you find things that feel like they turn a light on inside you.

D. <u>Mission and Vision board</u>. A few pages in my journal are dedicated to mapping out my mission and vision. *Mission* is your personal why: your north star. No matter what the road brings you will remain steadfast on this journey towards this thing because it is why you are here! *Vision* is what it could look, feel, sound, or taste like.

- Tip: Use this to dream big for your business too! Create the setting for your story: get detailed and keep this part to yourself for now. You don't need no hateration!

There is much more work put into my personal monastery at home, but journaling was a huge aspect of my healing. There is power in your story and seeing it unfold right before your eyes helps you sort out the important parts. It helps you see the truth of who you are. From there you can clearly decide what you need to do and where you need to go. For me it was adding in therapy, walking, and exercising more and changing my diet, often. I embraced my inner child and purchased hula hoops and skates. I began painting and doing yoga along with my meditation. I dived deeper into my spiritual practice and study and fully embraced my sexuality. I was more intentional about building my support system. I watched TV less, went on social media less. My healing and glow up sparked one of the novels I am writing—the self-help narrative, *Living on Purpose*. It's a part of my healing journal that I hope will share the power and light I found in myself as I blew away the dust left after my burnout.

It is a daily practice of being the you that you dream to be. Life will not stop trying to extinguish your light and burn out your candle but you're more powerful than you realize. Don't let the world tell you who you should be, how bright you can shine or what your limits are. There is power in healing and even more power in embracing your unique story. Be brave and rewrite your story and turn your pain into your superpower and let it ignite your purpose. Remember everything happens *for* you not *to* you. You are divinely perfect. Make space for the light that's ready to glow inside you and light up the world.

"Let nothing dim the light that shines from within."
-Maya Angelou

TAKEYLA BENTON

Takeyla Benton is a Madison, WI based, Black, queer woman, writer, mystic, tarot reader, Diversity Equity and Inclusion Analyst, and life coach committed to her own healing and harnessing the energy of trauma and transformation into the power to find life's purpose.

Website: takeylabenton.com

6

INTUITION IN BUSINESS
THE BEGINNING

I never thought I'd become self-employed, much less an entrepreneur. I grew up in a household where my dad had his own business, and still does forty years later. He was the breadwinner and everyone else fell in line.

Being assigned female at birth and always being rather unconventional, I never had any kind of representation, in my personal life or on screen, and therefore had no mental picture of what a queer entrepreneur would look like; it felt like an intangible impossibility.

But ten years into being employed, I'd had job after job, never quite fitting in, frequently put in environments that stressed me out, and I was constantly under-appreciated and under-utilised.

After dropping out of university, I decided to try my hand at hairdressing. I had only just escaped home, which was quite turbulent at the time, so I didn't want to go back. A friend had suggested I interview for a junior position at his salon, and there was the first instance of the thought *what have I got to lose?*

I didn't know it at the time, but that little voice in my head would prove to be the best resource I had on my entrepreneurial journey, far beyond the practical skills that are so often focused on by business coaches and the like. I had spent years being surrounded by old-school white businessmen who had very logical ideas about how to do business. Everything came down to money and there was no talk of one's life purpose, making a difference in the world, mental health, or the emotional challenges of creating something bigger than yourself.

I left my full-time job at the age of twenty-four and decided to strike out on my own. Despite my soon-to-be ex-boss, and a job agent I knew, warning me not to take the risk and to stay in employment, it was too late. The seed of the idea of being self-employed had taken root, and intuitively, I knew it just felt right. This was the first real exercise in trusting my intuition. Despite the fact I was terrified and didn't have anything in the way of a supportive entrepreneurial community at the time, I could feel my energy and creativity begin to soar.

Hairdressing, I knew, was not my life's passion, but it did give me the space I needed to breathe. The first time I ever booked a regular doctor's appointment and realised I didn't have to get permission from anyone or dodge a sexist manager who liked to speculate about where I was going this time, was a moment of great euphoria.

The first afternoon I had no clients and time to kill, I took myself to the cinema and felt both elated and naughty, like I was skipping school, hiding in the dark cinema and enjoying every minute of it. Along with my happiness and sense of freedom, my business grew, and within a year I was making the equivalent of my old full-time job whilst only working a quarter of the hours.

Things ticked along well for quite some time, but underneath the surface was the truth that hair and makeup was not my calling, and I was not in love with my business enough to ever make serious money out of it. This was where my traditional, masculine, and soulless introduction to business failed me; it did not prepare me for the fact that I could not manufacture motivation about things I did not deeply connect to. I was also struggling to manage undiagnosed PTSD (post-traumatic stress disorder), unhealthy relationships, and codependency. There frequently wasn't enough energy left over from all those draining things for me to think about making life bigger, or more complex.

I, still to this day, feel that I can only credit divine intervention for the evolution that needed to take place for me to become a bigger, more fulfilled version of myself. My hair and makeup business had given me the space I needed to tackle all the things keeping me stuck, burnt-out, and limited.

As I healed from burnout, I was beginning to become aware of how difficult some parts of my life were, and resentful that these things were taking up the time and energy I needed for myself to move forward. I had enough money to pay my bills, to socialise, and do the things I liked, but I knew instinctively that I would not be raking in large amounts of cash any time soon, because my heart was not in it enough.

My dad would frequently tell me about other people in my industry who'd created enormous wealth for themselves, yet I simply could not feel excited at the prospect of taking my business further.

The next breadcrumb the universe sent me was in the form of an audiobook by Dr. Judith Orloff, *Positive Energy Practices*. I'd come across an article of hers on the internet about Empaths and so profoundly recognised myself in her words, that I had to look her up, and there I found the book.

As I listened to her explain about being a sensitive person and describing the many types of Energy Vampires we may come across, I finally began to place relationships in my life within a measurable context. It allowed me to understand that people were walking around with their own emotional wounding, and that there was nothing I could do about it. It gave me the perspective I needed to begin to navigate relationships with both eyes open, and permission to step away from the people who did not add to my life, or who drained me. This audiobook was to be the beginning of an obsession and a hunger for an emotional education akin to water in a desert.

Once I'd gotten into a routine with work, a social life, and pushing myself forward for several years, I was able to move out into my own place and things kept getting better and better. I had really made friends with my intuition and had built it into my everyday life. I would meet new clients or friends and frequently began to intuit things about them that I couldn't possibly have otherwise known.

The first time I met one of my boxing coaches, the moment we shook hands, I was aware of him feeling low, despite his sunny disposition. I felt he was separated from his partner and two children and was struggling. This *knowing* was later confirmed in conversation with another boxer at the same club who knew him. I didn't often share these knowings with anyone as it was something strange and outside the remit of everything I'd been taught about the world.

The Big One

Then, the following new year, I found myself staring at the ticket sales page for an event in London I was dying to go to. The cheapest ticket was around £400, money I just didn't have to spare. And yet I kept going to look at this sales page almost every day, for weeks, accepting I couldn't go, but dreaming about it nonetheless. And then just a week before it was due to start, the organiser said to me, 'I want to sponsor someone to go, would you like to come?'

I gratefully accepted with tears in the back of my throat. What I couldn't have known was that this event was to be the place I received one of my scariest intuitions: that I would soon be closing my hair and makeup business and taking my advocacy on full-time.

The idea of closing the business that had given me my life back, even though I knew I was on borrowed time with it, was terrifying. Forget that this was a foreign concept, launching and conducting a business online; I had never met another trans or nonbinary person doing anything remotely similar.

The entire room at this event was filled with cisgender women, and a few cisgender men. As I listened to the many inspiring talks and trainings delivered over the course of the three-day event, I struggled so hard to imagine myself in their place or achieving anything like they had. It shouldn't have mattered, so I kept telling myself, but I really couldn't imagine a world in which anyone would be interested in anything I had to say, much less that it would be useful to anyone.

And yet, on the final day, as the organiser was asking if anyone wanted to talk to her about training as a coach, my hand shot up, much to my surprise. The intuition at this point was so strong, and I was only signing up for a conversation. After all, what did I have to lose?

Starting Again

My hairdressing business was naturally beginning to dry up, perfectly in-line with my energy surrounding it. As a Shaman friend of mine likes to remind me 'the old must die to make room for the new'. And I was scared again. The business that had sustained me for six years was coming to a close, with no guarantee of what was ahead. I really was going in blind this time. The only difference being that I had learned to really lean into my intuition, and by this point it was so easy to know when it was calling. Things fell into place; the right people turned up in my life; I felt happier and rejuvenated with an uptick of creativity. Every time.

I trained as an NLP Practitioner and Timeline Therapist that summer. The investment, which I couldn't afford, turned up at the very last minute. I had tried everything to pay for it and reached a dead-end every time. I gave up and became despondent as the deadline for enrolling came and went. And then out of the blue, the very next day, a friend had called me saying she had a feeling she needed to speak to me, then offered me the money over the phone. I began violently crying, which she asked me not to do.

'Send me your bank details; I'm getting off the phone now'. It still makes me laugh to this day.

In my head I believed that once I'd qualified, I'd need to start putting a business plan together, and then switch from hairdressing to coaching. At this point I'd started up three small companies, so felt fairly confident that I could do it and that the route to my new career was simple. F***, was I wrong!

That same year I had met someone and fallen for them. A nonbinary doctor of neuroscience, we both relished in our safe, queer bubble, and also enjoyed lots of in-depth discussions about the mind, perception, and beliefs. They had been offered a new job in Switzerland, and we had planned to move there together. A matter of weeks after finishing my NLP training, our relationship broke down. My housemate was moving as I thought I would be, too. And within a month I found myself with no house, no relationship, no business, and I'd just sold my car. Besides being devastated about the breakup, I remember angrily asking the universe 'well what now!?'.

'Leave,' was the response I got. Within a few months I was on a plane to Australia. Intuitively, it felt like, as in a video game, that I had completed the map of my home country. There were no more quests to complete. It made no sense, but riding on the surrender of heartbreak and nothing else tying me there, I thought to myself, 'what have I got to lose?'

Allergic to the possibility of being a cliché, I won't tell you that travelling was the best thing I've ever done. It was, however, the most unexpected chapter of my life to date, and it acquainted me with parts of myself I didn't know existed. And it pushed me so far outside my comfort zone I forgot what a comfort zone looked like. It tested my anxiety to the max, but it also showed me that I was capable of thriving, in the right environment. And then it showed me how badly I could fall when the right environment was snatched away from me, leading me to returning home after over a year of freedom, feeling extremely depressed and defeated.

Even in the depths of despair, finding myself back at my parents' house, my mental health shattered, there was still a sense deep within that something was afoot, and so I honoured where I was. I surrendered everything. The online community I'd been leading for six years, of some 20,000 LGBTQ+ people, I suspended. I handed over my support group to a trusted friend. I took a menial job. I walked two miles every night before bed in the still, cold night air. I got myself some anxiety medication from the doctor. And then I waited. I trusted that my intuition would tell me what was next, just like it had always done.

Some months went by without incident, life ticked over and I began to get used to the mundane. And just as I had stopped thinking about it, some green shoots within me began to sprout. I found myself tentatively taking a step back into my online community. Then as I was about to be furloughed from work, a friend invited me to start a podcast with them. Creativity, vision, and joy started to grow within me again.

In these last eighteen months I look back to the version of me that returned to the UK, broken and hopeless, and I thank the past me for the absolute strength and determination it took to persevere, despite how rough things looked on paper. I now have a podcast in its third season, a coaching practice that has helped people through so much: from PTSD, breakdowns, and career transformations, to supporting parents of trans and nonbinary children, to helping people start their own businesses. And my *Trans+ Gender Identity: A Guide for Beginners*, which came to me through the ether in the autumn of 2020, has since had hundreds of downloads and has helped people all over the world.

An evolution worth waiting for.

A note to my readers

As a pioneer, or the first in your family, social circle, or community to push the boundaries, your intuition is sometimes the only thing you've got. Acquaint yourself with it and begin to recognise the noticeably clear, positive signs that come with honouring it. It will bridge the gaps that others can't fill for you and it will take you the best route, even if on paper that looks pretty weird. Enjoy the journey and make sure your basic needs are met in order to lessen the pressure a little. And in case no one else tells you: Your existence and your purpose are divine. Spend time with people who know that, too. Don't waste time playing chess with pigeons.

HARRIS EDDIE HILL

Harris Eddie Hill (they/them or ey/em) is a trans nonbinary educator, inclusive coach, speaker, and seasoned podcaster, having appeared on many stages, podcasts, and events. Specialising in gender identity, they published Trans+ Gender Identity: A Guide for Beginners in September 2020, which has since had hundreds of downloads, across many countries. They have grown their online presence to some 35,000 people and have coached parents of trans and nonbinary children in order for their families and children to thrive. Harris is dedicated to the nurturing and accepting of the individual, and society, in all its multi-coloured glory. When each of us learns to fuel and shine our own light, together we can light up the world.

Website: mxharrishill.com
Contact: harris@mxharrishill.com
Instagram: @mxharrishill
Free Guide: Trans+ Guide: mxharrishill.com/pdf

7

THE POWER OF OPA!

I was thirty-eight, in the middle of a nasty divorce (since I had realized I was a lesbian), I had four growing kids to feed, and no marketable skills. What the hell was I going to do? After a ton of research and soul-searching, only two certainties emerged. I was meant to be my own boss and I'm a damn good storyteller, a trait inherited from my beloved dad.

I had survived conversion therapy and I knew I would survive building a business as well. I hired a business coach and she agreed that with the right roadmap, I could easily grow a consulting business. Then she uttered these words "You need credibility. You either need to write a book or do a TEDx talk." A quick conversation with other writers told me to go for the latter. They told me no publisher would consider me without at least 15,000 followers. I had maybe a hundred. TED talk it is!

The TEDx talk happened less than a year later and went viral! My business took off. Then, guess what happened? Literary agents started calling. I did my research, went with the best of the best and worked closely with her to write a beautifully crafted proposal, based on the story of my TEDx talk. Twelve months after my talk went live, I got a phone call from her.

"Your proposal is amazing. Every publishing house will want to publish this. But no one will buy it. I'm just telling you now. We're done."

WHAT?!

"You need at least 50,000 followers to get a book deal for this."

I couldn't wrap my head around it. My story had value, had merit, and yet, was unsellable? Because of follower counts?!

It finally sunk in. **Big publishers (and big brands) do not understand the LGBTQ+ market.** According to the publishing industry "Diversity Baseline Survey[1]" results in 2019: 76 percent of the industry overall is white, 74 percent are cis-women, and 81 percent are straight. Studies are showing that our population is changing, more and more people are identifying as LGBTQ+, yet we still can't find ourselves in modern channels, especially books.

Big Media has no idea how hungry we are for content (books, movies, magazines, TV shows, YouTube channels, Twitch shows) meant for us, by us, about us. They don't realize that 10k robot followers are worth nothing compared to just 500 raving queer fans. They don't understand how we never forget the first time we see a queer love story normalized, the first time we see a venture capitalist that looks like us, the first time we read a news story about a successful entrepreneur (who also happens to be LGBTQ+). It changes our lives, and we never forget it.

Big Media might not get it. But I did. I knew I could create a business, sell books, and make money, no matter how much they underestimated me.

So, I did.

But what about you? What can you do if you need that audience count up, you need some serious income (like NOW), and you have, I don't know, say one-hundred followers? I got you, fam.

It's time to OPA!

Besides being a fabulous word to yell while dancing at Greek weddings, OPA (Other People's Audiences) is also an acronym that's going to change your business forever.

You, my friend, are going to grow a massive business simply offering value to Other People's Audiences. And Imma tell you exactly how to do it.

"But why, Elena Joy? This sounds intimidating and uncomfortable, and I need to know WHY first. Of all the ways to grow my business, why OPA?"

Two words.

Content and **Credibility.**

Content is what you offer to your audience, hopefully of value. Specifically, this content is: social media posts, video footage, email newsletters, blog posts, etc. We all need content as we all need an excuse to be in front of our audience. But constant content creation is a one-way ticket to burn out.

Content needs to be multi-purposed. Let me give you an example. I found a podcast I really wanted to get on. Was it the biggest one? Not even close. But I knew their audience was filled with adoring fans who shared many of my passions, as well as a demographic I hadn't had much access to. I secured my interview, showed up on time, gave great responses, and had a blast.

From that experience:

- I did an IG post about how excited I was for the interview.
- I shared a behind-the-scenes (BTS) IG story as we were getting the audio and video ready.
- I did an IG post, a FB post, and a Tweet once it went live.
- I also did a workplace-focused post on LinkedIn.
- I summarized the interview for my email newsletter and included a link.
- I wrote a blog post about it.
- I created four different quote graphics, used them as graphics in the blog post and then pinned them on Pinterest.

Not only did we give valuable content to a peer's audience, but we also spread the content around to our core audience. No burnt-out queer entrepreneurs on my watch!

Credibility is the secret sauce that makes your content 10x more valuable. As humans, we inherently value something more if it's suggested by someone we admire. If someone hands me the mic, their audience immediately feels like what I have to say must be at least a little important.

By offering value to someone else's audience, you're also enhancing your credibility to all your clients and audience. By increasing your credibility, you are increasing the likelihood that your audience will consider you the expert and worth an investment of their time, energy, and money.

My biggest love for OPA is the laziness it allows. Marketing was not my strong suit, and, in the beginning, I couldn't afford a marketing expert. It was really, really hard for me to gather my own audience, so being able to show up for an audience that someone else has already gathered for me?! Sign me up!

Ready to leverage Other People's Audiences? OPA!!
Break out your notebook, kids. It's time to brainstorm.

First, who do you serve? How do you serve them? What problems do you solve? Get really clear here on the value you provide and to whom. Then ask yourself, "What would feel good to provide in the form of a talk or workshop?" You can come up with two to three options depending on your niche (you'll use this in your pitches later).

Second, who are your adjacent peers? Not the ones offering the exact same services and clients as you, but who has an audience with a makeup similar to yours but you're solving different problems?

For example, my nonprofit supports LGBTQ+ families. Adjacent peers for us have been:

- Another nonprofit who raises funds to puts LGBTQ+ centered children's books in teachers' classrooms (https://www.prideandlessprejudice.org/)
- Numerous coming out coaches

- Numerous parenting coaches
- Queer dating coaches
- Queer financial coaches
- Photographers who specialize in queer weddings and families
- A parent coach who specializes in supporting parents of trans kids (https://www.mxharrishill.com/)

I can offer value to every single one of those audiences, even though my product is not solving their original problem. Oftentimes, my solution is for a problem they didn't know they had. In turn, my audience can receive value from those peers, as well. Hence, an exchange is not a hard sell.

This is not a "get a captive audience and pitch to them" type of strategy, this has to be from a desire to serve the people who need you. The confidence comes from knowing that the sales will come when the value aligns with the audience. If you are pitching people that aren't aligned or if it looks like you're just trying to piggyback off of someone else's hard work, ain't nobody buying it. Yourself included.

In your notebook, list out at least twenty-five of your peer audiences. Right this second, schedule two hours a week to devote to introducing yourself and pitching the idea of offering value to their audience. You already have your list, so it'll be super easy to just go down the list during your two hours.

Suggest a medium to present to their audience that makes sense: whether it's an IG Live, a webinar, a takeover day on their socials, or an actual live, in person presentation - whatever works for both of you and is FUN!

VALUE! IS! KING! HERE! So you have to be very clear what value you bring and WHY they should partner with you. There is no need to pursue perfection, the goal is clarity of the value.

Lastly, after you've sent the emails or DMs, schedule another hour-long block of time three to five days later for following up. The most successful people need a second follow up to really get their attention. Then you can let it go knowing you did everything you could.

Podcasts

There are **so** many podcasts and when you're first starting, your only expectation can be for credibility and content. You're going to post content around it and it will be mildly impressive to your audience that someone else handed you the microphone, no matter what size podcast it is. Small podcasts can easily be found through:

- Facebook groups for podcast hosts
- Google searches - find aligned audience through keywords from your ideal avatar profile. Podcasts with fewer than fifty ratings are usually on the hunt for SMEs (subject matter experts). That's you. You're the expert.
- Industry secret: Who is that person in your industry that makes you green with envy? Who makes you wish you had their audience? Find out what podcasts they've been on. If your idol is huge and speaks to massive audiences, you'll have to search back to the beginning of their career for the smaller ones.

Effectively leveraging podcasts to build your business is a subject area that can't be fully explored in a single chapter. It's worth doing some of your own research to learn the best ways to secure the interview, what to do and not do during the interview, and how to sustain a relationship with a quality host.

Speaking to Associations

These are groups of professional people that gather regularly to network and offer support to each other. They need content and value, which means they need YOU.

Let's say you are a women's leadership coach. You teach women how to use their voice powerfully and confidently to achieve their goals. Guess who needs you to teach them for 30-45 minutes?

- The association of women lawyers in your area
- The association of women accountants in your area
- The association of women dentists in your area
- We can go on, but you get the idea.

Local, regional, and national associations are all looking for presenters and these days, the majority of those presentations are done online. No pants!

Pitch, please!

It's time to be working on your pitch. This is the initial email that you'll send to the meeting coordinator and/or podcast host. Convince them that you have great value to offer their audience, and you're in!

A great speaking pitch has a few distinct parts.

- An **introduction** that shows them that you know and value their mission and their audience. This step is crucial and so many of your competitors skip right over it. We all know those people, right? They somehow got your email address and they're trying to sell you something without any idea of who you are and what you need. Don't be that person. Do fifteen minutes of research and show them that you're invested in their success.
- Your **value proposition**. This paragraph should lead with what could be the title of your talk, what problem it's solving, and how other people have found it valuable. Here's an example from one of my association pitches.

In this presentation we focus on how organizations, particularly leaders and managers, can create safety and belonging for LGBTQ employees. During our conversation, I'd share with listeners a concept we teach called The Mental Boardroom™. It's a strategy to create increased inclusion in an authentic and often life-changing way.

After a recent speaking engagement, one audience member reached out to us about how The Mental Boardroom™ process changed his life - allowing him to release internalized homophobia he's held onto for decades (You can read more about his aha moment on our blog).

- **List of takeaways**. Time is everyone's most valuable resource these days. By clearly listing what their audience members are going to walk away with, you're telling them that your information is valuable and worth their time. The takeaways need to begin with verbs, nothing passive. My example from the preceding pitch (emphasis added):

In this presentation, we cover a lot of rich territory so that audience members:

- *Know the difference between an active LGBTQ+ ally and a performative ally.*
- *Recognize what vocabulary to use (and not use!) with colleagues, coworkers, friends, and family.*
- *Leave with a keen understanding of unconscious bias - where it comes from and how to address it when it shows up.*
- **Next steps**. Lastly, we spell out exactly what we want them to do. Is it clicking on our scheduling link? Respond to this email? Most people are excited to help others, but they often just don't know the clear and easy method. Be clear regarding the next step you want them to take.

I strongly suggest that you batch your work where you can and utilize templated emails (with customization in the intro) to save yourself some time.

But how do I get OPA to buy?

Few audiences will be warm and ready for your pitch. Most audiences need you to be minimally salesy, which you probably prefer anyway. You don't have to say, "Buy my offer!" three times throughout your talk. Anyone who tells you that is probably not as successful as they're pretending to be.

Selling from stage tips:

1. Make sure your freebie offer (often called a "lead magnet") has its own domain name. Mine is www.AllyQuiz.com. My mentor's freebie is www.BookCorporateGigs.com. With its own domain name, you can casually mention it during your talk and often you'll watch people immediately go there and sign up. It's not your website per se so it doesn't feel high pressure, it's just an offer of value that you've already shown them they need.

2. Use a few examples of other people that have used your services in your talk. This casually communicates that they need your services as well. "One client of mine had ABC problem, sound familiar? When we solved it, they experienced XYZ."

3. Near the end, clearly ask people to connect with you on your favorite medium. If I'm speaking to families, I say "Connect with me on Instagram @pridejoyfoundation." If I'm speaking to associations or business groups I say "Connect with me on LinkedIn. Elena Joy Thurston." Make it easy on them!

By working this system, continuing to refine and improve, you WILL find mass momentum. If you've done a good job and maintained connections, word of mouth is going to boost you to your next level in business. The absolute key to finding this momentum is relationships, they can make or break you.

Wondering if you should create some content this morning, or connect with past event organizers? Connect! Wondering if you should write another email newsletter tomorrow, or comment and connect with peer audiences? Connect! Wondering if you should send a handwritten thank you note to the association you just spoke to? You know the answer.

Ready to toss your cookies at the thought of being on stage?

If the idea of speaking in front of audiences makes you want to throw up a little, there's a reason. Literally the only fears we are born with is a fear of falling and a startle reflex from loud noises. Everything else is learned. We all feel sensation around visibility but not all of us are held back by it.

Free yourself to leverage OPA by finding out the source of your sensation. One of the best resources for finding power and strength in visibility is the book *Step Into Your Moxie* by Alexia Vernon. So Powerful!

Oftentimes for LGBTQ+ entrepreneurs, **the fear of visibility is very real and very valid.**

When we grow up as a marginalized person, we are constantly doubting our right to take up space, our right to use our voice in a powerful way, and especially our right to experience success. We tend to look for others like us that have already figured it out, almost like a permission slip we need signed.

Guess what? **You are that person.** You are the pioneer LGBTQ+ entrepreneur who is paving the way and setting the stage that our next generation of change-makers will look up to. So, consider that permission slip signed and dated! Get on the bus! Next stop, financial freedom!

ELENA JOY THURSTON

Elena Joy Thurston is an inspirational LGBTQ speaker, trainer, and founder of the nonprofit Pride and Joy Foundation. A Mormon mom of four who lost her marriage, her church, and her community when she came out as a lesbian, Elena's viral TEDx talk on surviving conversion therapy has been viewed 40,000+ times and landed her media and speaking opportunities with ABC, CBS, FOX, Penn State, and Michael's. Elena Joy recently launched Pride and Joy Publishing, the only publisher of solely LGBTQ+ empowerment and business books.

Website: PrideandJoyFoundation.org
Instagram: @pridejoyfoundation

8

BRINGING PEOPLE TOGETHER, ONE BOOK AT A TIME

S tories are powerful – and intuitively human. Sharing our own stories can influence culture, teach new perspectives, provide insight, and allow children to better understand themselves and others. Stories bring us together. Let me start with my own.

Having a queer daughter who struggled to come to terms with her sexuality, I've often thought about how her childhood could have been more LGBTQ-inclusive. When my two children were in preschool and early elementary school, I spent endless hours reading books to them; but as I reflect upon our favorite titles, I realize that I did not introduce my children to the diversity in books that I had hoped for.

Besides being the mother of a daughter who identifies as queer, I am also a former educator. I have taught in various settings, including preschools, libraries, and music groups for upwards of twenty-five years. Through all my years of working with children and raising them, I have seen firsthand the positive effects of inclusive and representative education.

But my daughter Becca never knew any LGBTQ folks in her childhood; the media was her lifeline. She really connected to TV shows with LGBTQ-inclusive storylines like *Glee, Pretty Little Liars,* and *Modern Family,* and with the help of those shows, she came out as queer.

I see now how having that representation helped her figure that out for herself. I often wonder what her life would have been like without that representation, and the more I thought about that, the more I realized how much having LGBTQ-inclusive literature in the classroom would have helped her. I kept thinking if we could just get these children's books into the younger grades, starting with preschool, we could normalize inclusivity amongst all children, teachers, and parents.

As an educator myself, the idea of LGBTQ representation in preschools and elementary schools just made so much sense to me. The benefits of an inclusive education for young children are astounding: Children who identify with marginalized communities feel more accepted in the classroom, more trusting of school staff, administration, and peers, and more ready to learn in a space that they feel acknowledges and celebrates them. Their peers benefit by engaging with stories unfamiliar to them, as well, thus teaching them the important skills of empathy and inclusion.

After speaking to a queer second grade teacher about what resources she uses in her classroom, I began to do some research and see what kind of LGBTQ-inclusive books had been published for young children. There were many more than I ever imagined. Some of my favorites include: *Heather Has Two Mommies* by Lesléa Newman, an iconic book about a little girl with two moms where her family situation is discussed simply and positively; *It Feels Good To Be Yourself* by Theresa Thorn, a sweet, straightforward exploration of gender identity provides young readers the vocabulary to discuss this topic; and *Pride: The Story of Harvey Milk and the Rainbow Flag,* by Rob Sanders, which traces the life of the Gay Pride Flag with gay-rights activist Harvey Milk and designer Gilbert Baker.

I, eventually, narrowed down the list to fourteen books and began to ask some teachers I knew if they would like free LGBTQ-inclusive books for their classrooms. I was happy to find many teachers who wanted to use the books, and I was thrilled to have the chance to support these teachers, many of whom did not have the funding from their schools to buy these books themselves. Through this process, I also realized that many teachers, who are both LGBTQ and allies, did not know that there were so many LGBTQ-inclusive resources for Pre-K and elementary classrooms.

That was the beginning of Pride and Less Prejudice (PLP), a non-profit organization I created in November 2019 to provide free, LGBTQ-inclusive books to classrooms from Pre-K to third grade. Since I started this organization with my two daughters, PLP has raised over $32,000 and donated more than 2,000 books to classrooms in forty-three U.S. states and five Canadian provinces. We have received grant support from the Tegan and Sara Foundation and The Pollination Project, as well as many individual donations from people who share the passion for what we do.

In addition to providing LGBTQ-inclusive books for teachers, we also support teachers with free teacher resource guides, which accompany each featured book, and professional development workshops. We continue to support our teachers further with author read-alouds and educational and experience-driven blog posts about the importance of inclusion.

It takes a village; I could never have reached this point without my amazing team of twelve passionate volunteers from across the country, comprised of both members of the queer community and allies. This is absolutely beyond what I had ever hoped. Never in my wildest dreams did I imagine PLP would have such a broad reach. Looking back on PLP's journey, I realized we learned many lessons along the way.

We experienced firsthand the power of the LGBTQ activism on social media. When we first started, my daughter Becca reconnected with LGBTQ activist and author Kristin Russo, who co-founded the LGBTQ youth organization Everyone Is Gay. In 2014, Becca acted as Kristin's tour manager and planned a book tour to promote her book, *This is a Book for Parents of Gay Kids*. Kristin has a large following on social media, and immediately agreed to share our initiative.

Becca also reached out to folks at the LGBTQ media advocacy organization, GLAAD, where she had interned in 2015, and the organization agreed to share PLP with its more than 475,000 followers. Additionally, Becca attended Smith College, where she met a large number of LGBTQ folks, and shared our work on some of the alum Facebook pages. Slowly but surely, we began to receive book requests and donations from all over the country, and even Canada!

What initially gave us the biggest jump was our post on Pantsuit Nation in April 2020. Pantsuit Nation is a private Facebook group that was started in 2016 to support Hillary Clinton's presidential campaign. Now with over three million members and having joined with the women's organization Supermajority, Pantsuit Nation X Supermajority has become a place for members to post personal stories. Becca posted about PLP in the group several months earlier, but it wasn't until the last day of April that her post was approved. Almost overnight, the post got more than 3,000 likes and again, people began to request books and make donations.

Even during a global health crisis, people still wanted to come together to support a common cause. In fact, perhaps in part because of the pandemic, we got more requests for books than donations from the folks that interacted with us on Pantsuit Nation. We learned that schools were lacking the funds to provide materials that are considered outside of their curriculum, and teachers were overwhelmed by the combination of both virtual and in-person learning. Unfortunately, we know from experience that the stories of LGBTQ people are not always prioritized when it comes to selecting classroom reading materials - but this in no way lessens the importance of these inclusive materials. We also know that the pandemic exacerbated educational inequities and will shape the educational and personal outcomes of an entire generation. Now more than ever, we needed to ensure that LGBTQ visibility and acceptance were present in educational spaces. We needed to find a way to fund the demand.

With that in mind, we wanted to harness the power of queer visibility and media representation to bring attention to our mission. We decided to create a celebrity campaign video to share our message and raise money to support the demand. We reached out to many LGBTQ celebrities, asking them to speak about the importance of LGBTQ media representation, and what it would have meant to them to have had LGBTQ-inclusive children's books in their classrooms.

After we received the footage, my younger daughter Ally, who studied Arts for Social Change at Franklin & Marshall College, created a three-minute campaign video for us. In the end, we were amazed that thirteen LGBTQ celebrities, including Adam Rippon, Tig Notaro, Darryl Stephens, Harvey Guillén, and Nicole Maines, agreed to record a video for us.

Here are just a few quotes from the video:

"LGBTQ representation is important, especially for young people, because it shows them that they are not alone." ~Nicole Maines, actress (*Supergirl*)

"It really is important to have LGBTQ characters represented, especially with younger kids, and while their minds are being shaped, and to tell them that it's okay, and we live in a world with different people, and their stories are just as valid and important." ~Harvey Guillén, actor (*What We Do In the Shadows*)

"Seeing characters whose experiences reflect our own affirms that our feelings are valid, and that we too, deserve to be loved." ~Darryl Stephens, actor (*Noah's Arc*)

LISTENING to the stories of others was so moving. Having the celebrities speak to their real-life experiences was so important and proved, yet again, why LGBTQ representation matters, and brought us a base of compassionate supporters. We started to create a PLP family.

It never hurts to ask. Our motto was literally, "Reach for the stars!" The only thing that could happen is that people would say no. We also experienced firsthand the importance of social media and saw how celebrities and influencers can increase the visibility of a cause.

Our celebrity video landed us some incredible media coverage in *USA Today*, *The Advocate*, *GO Magazine*, *Tagg Magazine* and several more, which allowed us to raise more than $10,000, but also skyrocketed the number of book requests we received from teachers.

Early on, we also started to speak to the authors of these incredible stories as we wanted to learn more about them. We created an interview series called *Meet The Authors*, and more recently, we created #TellingQueerStories, a campaign video in which the authors of our featured books share their personal stories. Not only did we see that the stories in the books are important, but so are the stories of the authors' lives and the experiences that motivated them to write these stories. Here are a few quotes from our featured authors:

"I would hope that these books let kids who will one day understand and recognize their identities if they don't already, see themselves in books, and allow other children, who aren't in the community, understand us, me, better because they fall in love with a character who's like me."
~Rob Sanders, author (*Stonewall: A Building. An Uprising. A Revolution.*)

"When a child that is LGBTQ or has LGBTQ family members finds themselves in a book or in a story, they learn that their own stories are worth telling. And when a child that is not LGBTQ

reads a story, and it has characters that are, they learn that people who are LGBTQ have stories that are worth listening to, and that LGBTQ people are worth including in their own life."
~Mark Loewen, author, (*What Does A Princess Really Look Like?*)

OVER THE LAST TWO YEARS, we have been fortunate to speak with many of the teachers requesting LGBTQ-inclusive books from us and continue to hear their stories as well. Many of the teachers ask for specific books as they are wanting to support a particular child in their classroom. We are proud that we make our donations very personal and try to tailor what we send.

A teacher from Canada shared, "We have several gender nonconforming students at school, as well as a few [families with] same-sex couple[s]. I know that to see themselves represented is very powerful." Another teacher from Canada shared, "I think by reading and discussing these books, we are giving space for discussions and sending the message that we include and accept everyone in our school."

A teacher from the U.S. said, "I was so thrilled to receive a donation from PLP to read with my preschool students. I am so happy to teach children about being inclusive and having LGBTQ people as part of our culture's fabric from a young age. In this way, we are not really just teaching, we are exposing them to another normal part of life."

All of these stories combined—the celebrities, authors, teachers, and allies—continue to create this bond. The stories are what make people care and are what continue to bring us together. I realize now that Becca did not have the opportunity to see LGBTQ-inclusive representation in books until much later in her life. Through Pride and Less Prejudice, I am determined to provide the next generation of children with this positive representation in the classroom, from the beginning of their education.

Ultimately, I hope it will be the children's stories that will push this work forward. I can't wait for the day when I hear a student later in life share, "I remember when I was in second grade, I heard my teacher read the book, *Born Ready* by Jodie Patterson, and I saw myself in that character and I connected in a way I had never had the opportunity to do before."

Reflecting back on the importance of LGBTQ-inclusive children's books, Tony Award-nominated actress Lauren Patten shared, "If I had seen that, and had it been normalized much earlier in my life, who knows? Who knows when I would have been able to recognize that part of my identity? It would have been really special; I hope that for other kids."

LISA B. FORMAN

Lisa Forman (she/her) is the Founder of Pride and Less Prejudice. She has been teaching children music in preschools, libraries, and music groups, and through private piano lessons for more than twenty-five years. She has a B.A. in music and psychology from Boston University and an M.A. in music therapy from New York University. She has been married to her husband Sal for thirty-two years, has two grown daughters, Becca and Ally, and a labradoodle named Penny. Together, PLP has become a family labor of love. In Lisa's spare time, she is also a mixed media artist and loves to travel.

Website: prideandlessprejudice.org
Facebook: @prideandlessprejudice
Instagram: @prideandlessprejudice
Twitter: @lessprejudice

9

(LGBTQ+) NETWORKING AS YOUR SECRET WEAPON

Networking can be an intimidating word for anyone. I am a professional who graduated with a digital marketing degree in 2017 and a master's degree in 2020. I grew up in the digital age where information overload was the norm. After graduation, the last thing on my mind was to follow the advice of career advisors when they told me that, in order to get a job, I needed to "network, network, network!" Those words couldn't have sounded more unappealing, intimidating, and insignificant to me at the time.

There's something about the word *networking* that makes it feel less personable, and I believe it's a result of how people in authority teach us how to do it. Throughout college, my career advisors taught me not to get political when networking. But how do you avoid getting political when disclosing your sexuality or gender identity can get you fired in certain circumstances? What is professional when some consider your very existence as unprofessional?

LGBTQ+ people, in any new social interaction, ultimately must decide if they feel comfortable enough to out themselves to their interlocutor. It's no different in professional settings. This internal debate in every new interaction becomes even more complicated if you're an LGBTQ+ person of color. All of this flies in the face of traditional tips for networking.

None of the advice of my career counselors ever spoke to me as a bisexual, non-binary person of color. As a result, I felt fundamentally misunderstood by the concept of networking until I decided to start my own business as a queer digital marketer who helps other LGBTQ+ entrepreneurs and entrepreneurs of color take up space in their industries. During the first year of networking and building my own business, Marketing by Rocio, I've learned that many of the unspoken rules of business etiquette are different for LGBTQ+ folks. There was not a guidebook for me when I started, but through time, research, and hands-on experience, my view on networking shifted from a nihilist perspective to an empowering one with a focus on marginalized identities.

From here on out, let us think of networking at its core as just *connecting* with people. History proves that LGBTQ+ people know how to connect and organize. The words you're reading right now are further evidence of this. We organized to write and distribute this book, and you are reading it now to make the most of the resources we present to you. We are a resourceful community, and our influence knows no bounds, no matter how many times society tries to diminish us.

The fact is, LGBTQ+ entrepreneurs *are* taking up space already, whether or not we are making our LGBTQ+ identity a core part of our business identity, so we should do so with pride and extend a helping hand while we're at it. Other LGBTQ+ people *want* us to thrive. *I*, we the authors of this book, want you to thrive. Know that at the end of the day, you have a community behind you, cheering you on. You deserve to be here and connect with anyone you want. Your business is needed, and you have something valuable to offer.

Therein lies the major difference between networking within the LGBTQ+ community and networking outside of it: With LGBTQ+ people, you don't feel silenced but empowered. When I walk into a room full of LGBTQ+ professionals, I know that I don't need to hide any part of my story. That doesn't mean that the people I talk to will agree with me on every political stance. The point is that I can bypass the usual barriers that lead to me questioning my legitimacy as a person. Because I know that, on some level, the people in that space share lived experiences with me, and that makes all the difference.

UNTIL FINISHING graduate school in 2020, I felt silenced in traditional networking events, so I avoided them altogether. I felt like any contribution I made would ruffle feathers and compromise my barely-started career. I struggled with feeling like I couldn't be openly queer and voice my anti-capitalist and anti-racist views. But after graduating, I could no longer avoid the fact that networking was necessary to enter the job market *somehow*. Not only that, I also felt that I had to figure out how to balance the reality that I needed to make a living, knowing that networking was my golden ticket for that, with this deep feeling of inadequacy that I felt as an openly bisexual non-binary person of color.

I found the strength to dive into networking by promising myself one thing: I wouldn't be quiet about what I believed in. I focused on tips and resources from the countless workshops I'd attended over the years. I thought back to meetings with career advisors before setting out on my journey; I spent hours optimizing my professional social network profiles and learning how digital platforms work. I did all of this, still struggling to figure out how to be myself without compromising my career. Finally, after countless nights of scrolling through professional social media feeds, reaching out to people haphazardly, and optimizing my profiles, a switch flipped.

I saw a viral post from one of my connections on a professional networking site. The post in question was about their toddler interrupting their online video meeting. It was a typical post for the time: COVID-19 pandemic-induced content about working from home. It exemplified how the home couldn't be separated from work, even if it never actually was, no matter how hard American work culture tries to make it so.

I recognized a trend in these professional digital spaces: People from my network talked about their weddings, anniversaries, spouses, and even babies. They were talking about their *lives* with seemingly no hesitation. I realized this was also an opportunity. I saw all my cisgender, heterosexual connections talking about their lives and knew there had to be LGBTQ+ people out there doing the same, so I hatched a plan to reach them.

Over the course of a year, I attended a handful of online LGBTQ+ networking events. I started with Lesbians Who Tech, an organization that champions LGBTQ+ women in the technology industry, and then TransTech, an organization that does the same for trans people of all genders. Both organizations offered virtual days-long summits, where I made valuable connections.

As a digital marketer, an integral part of my job is tech-based, and I occasionally dabble in coding as a result, so these groups spoke to me. They allowed me to tap into my potential as a digital marketer and think outside the box with my career development. I didn't feel like a pawn trying to win brownie points every time I attended an event. I just felt like myself.

When you think about where you should network, different things might come to mind. You may picture physical networking events, career and job fairs, or inviting someone to connect somewhere online. However, I deliberately haven't discussed networking in a singular place, digital or physical, because fostering human-to-human connections transcends location. Use the tools and resources at your disposal, whether that is a search engine, a social network, or good old word-of-mouth, to find your people.

While digital platforms are ephemeral, our community is evergreen. I can detail the mechanics of my networking strategy for the past year, but who knows how obsolete some of those tips can be even twelve months after this book is published. If you want to explore up-to-date marketing strategies to optimize your reach in digital spaces, contact me on any of the platforms mentioned in my bio to discuss. Just remember: No matter what platform you're on, your reach is virtually limitless because, as the saying goes, LGBTQ+ people have always existed, and so they can be found. What you do to reach them is just a matter of gadgetry.

Discovering LGBTQ+ people in professional spaces just *existing* without explanation made me realize that I could do the same. Through online groups, hashtags, webinars, and other unique resources, I found that the feelings of inadequacy and secrecy melted away when engaging with professional communities of LGBTQ+ people, especially when said communities housed other people of color. When you find other individuals with shared experiences, you likely bypass the question of if your interlocutor believes you deserve fundamental rights or if today's going to be the day that your very existence is deemed debatable.

None of this is to say that there can't be unsafe environments when you're around LGBTQ+ people. There are many aspects of one's identity, from class to physical ability, that determine their risk level walking into any environment. This is where boundaries come in. An excellent place to start is to remember that networking doesn't have to occur all at once. Often, networking can be accomplished best when executed sustainably, allowing you to avoid burnout early on. Sustainable networking can mean deleting the mail application from your computer's dock, so you don't feel tempted to check it several times a day. It can mean designating days of no social media. Maintaining a viable work-life balance is not always easy, but making an effort is crucial to avoiding fatigue.

As I began networking within my communities, I learned how important it is to set boundaries. For me, boundaries include unfollowing and cutting off anyone who does not make me feel safe, valued, or understood in online spaces. And sometimes, it takes burning out to learn and establish your boundaries because we all navigate oppressive systems differently on an individual level. All LGBTQ+ people are different, but the same cisgender, heteronormative patriarchal society rules us all.

We all experience some level of risk when we decide to walk into a professional setting and openly disclose our identities, so take the time to understand what boundaries you need. Unfortunately, it's so easy to get swept up in hustle culture and feel as though you have to constantly grind and prove yourself in an attempt to seem productive. I don't buy into that, and I wish fewer people would. Rest is just as critical as proven success.

It took me years to actively create space for other marginalized voices, particularly those of LGBTQ+ individuals and people of color and allow myself the same space in both physical and digital places. As a digital marketing professional with years of experience in the fashion industry, I felt unseen and misunderstood in seemingly every space I occupied—my fashion internships, all of the magazines and social media content I grew up consuming—to the point that I felt estranged from my own communities. So, when I finally had the opportunity to *make* my own space as a queer brand strategist for LGBTQ+ entrepreneurs and entrepreneurs of color, I realized that people like me are everywhere; I just had to find them. That's where networking comes in.

When I was still a bright-eyed college student years ago, the concept of networking sounded, frankly, fake and dishonest, but that view has since changed. Authority figures in my life instructed me how to say the right things, smile, exemplify "good" body language, label myself a team player, remain apolitical, the works. It was a subtle game; at least, that's how I saw it. It's all to get what you want: a job, a decent living, *success*.

Now, years later, I understand that networking doesn't have to be disingenuous. It's just *connecting* with people, which is what we already do on a day-to-day basis with everyone in our lives. When I took the leap and decided to focus my networking efforts on LGBTQ+ people, I realized that what I was missing in my previous efforts were *empowerment* and authentic community. This epiphany played a significant role in mending my relationship with networking because seeing other LGBTQ+ people being themselves in professional settings permitted me to do the same. *That's* our superpower as a community.

As an entrepreneur, it's best to find and nurture a network that will support you in whatever way you present yourself. You don't even have to put your LGBTQ+ identity at the forefront of your personal brand or business. As LGBTQ+ entrepreneurs, we are creating a space that has rarely been tapped into before. We don't have time, and historically don't have the patience, to wait for our oppressors to give us the resources we need. We can provide that for ourselves just fine. And if done right, networking with the right people can give you the confidence to do what you, as a person, want to accomplish in the world.

Networking as an LGBTQ+ entrepreneur includes connecting with others on your own terms and honoring your boundaries. It comes with an understanding that social media will come and go but that *real* connections are resilient. Understanding how networking works for you personally and setting boundaries within your professional life will be gamechangers when exploring other business strategies you find in this book, whether or not your LGBTQ+ identity coincides with your business identity or brand. By coming together as the LGBTQ+ community, we can build our inner confidence and tackle the world in whatever context, professional or not. When you're LGBTQ+, networking is your secret weapon. All you have to do is use it.

ROCIO SANCHEZ

Rocio Sanchez is a non-binary brand strategist and multilingual digital marketing specialist who believes LGBTQ+ entrepreneurs and entrepreneurs of color should take up space in their industries. As a business consultant, Rocio helps these entrepreneurs stand out on different digital platforms with impactful marketing strategies influenced by their lived experiences and multicultural education. They hold a bachelor's degree in marketing from the Fashion Institute of Technology and a master's degree in fashion studies from Parsons Paris. They are originally from New York City and the Dominican Republic and have lived in Paris, France for three years. They speak English, Spanish, and French fluently and have a personal goal of becoming a polyglot.

Website: https://marketingbyrocio.com
Instagram: @marketingbyrocio
LinkedIn: @rocio-d-sanchez

10

MARKETING THROUGH AUTHENTICITY

I remember as a young girl, stories were the thing that held me together when nothing else could. I was raised in a deeply conservative, southern Christian family where there were definite ideas around what was right, what was wrong, and what was unacceptable. In that kind of environment, sameness is celebrated, and you are either doing it how they said and following the crowd, or you are going to hell.

But books were the place where the heroes went at it alone. They followed a different path or went against the crowd, chased dreams others said were impossible, or dared to speak their truth no matter the cost. As a young queer girl living in a world that told me everything about who I was and what I wanted for my life was wrong, those stories were my salvation.

It's no wonder, then, that after going to college for social work and working as a case manager for a year, I left all of that to become a photographer. While social work is deeply tied to humanity, I fell in love with the way photography allowed me to connect with so many different folks and to tell their stories. Photography was where anyone had the space to be seen and where stories came to life in living, vibrant color. And I loved everything about it.

Starting, growing, and marketing a business were all things I had no experience in though. We aren't really taught that working for ourselves is an option in our modern education system. So many years were spent trying all kinds of things, listening to other people, and learning how they became successful. I made more mistakes than I care to admit but one of the biggest I see looking back was how much I strived to do things the way others did. I so desperately wanted to be successful that I never stopped to ask what success looked like *to me*, and not how others defined it. I joined Facebook groups and masterminds and made friends with other photographers and desperately tried to do what they said worked for them. While my business grew, it never was more than someone else's idea of what a business ought to be.

At the time, I was editing in a trendy matte style, but not because I liked the way it looked. I realized I was only doing it because I thought being trendy was the only way to be successful. I was showing very few LGBTQ+ photos because I was afraid of what potential clients might think. I was posting captions on social media that were so fake and forced but I believed I had to do it that way. I had ideas of ways to market that I never followed through on because no one had ever done those things before. Unintentionally, I had become the business owner who did things with the approach of sameness I had been taught as a child. If I just did things the way I was told to, eventually I would be success-ful, right? But by whose standards?

It is far easier to follow the path that others have. While being gay, for many of us, goes against the "normal" path, being that type of authentic in our businesses is often harder. We define success by the standards of someone else, defaulting to the methods and practices of those we think have "made it" but so often they are successful because they did something different than the norm. They dared to try things that seemed crazy, and some-times they worked, sometimes they didn't. This resonated with me because this is what I had seen every hero in my childhood books go through. And I decided one random day that I was done trying to assimilate or contort myself and my business into something I am not.

I began to change my editing to the full-of-color, bright, and vibrant style I am now known for. I stopped forcing my social media to "follow the rules" of perfect captions and expertly timed postings and instead started sharing whatever I wanted to in the moment. My business came out as LGBTQ+ owned. I started unfollowing business Facebook groups. I put distance between myself and folks I viewed as mentors because I knew that if I wanted to find **my** voice, I had to remove all the other noise from around me. I stopped listening to the business strategies of others and instead leaned into trying the crazy ideas that came to me in the middle of the night. Without all the noise, I began to see how capable I was. It wasn't a linear growth; I had to often unlearn the old habits of following the crowd and learn to follow my own voice and ideas instead, but year after year my business grew.

That's not to say that marketing strategies are bad or that none of them work. You are, after all, reading a book about business strategies! But there isn't *just one way* to be successful and in the same vein, success can look and mean different things to different people! This, I think, is the biggest piece of marketing advice I can give you. Marketing is about all the activities a company does to sell a product or service to a consumer and there are literally thousands of things you can do. So often though we default to what someone told us worked, never stopping to consider what else is out there or if those methods of marketing are what resonate with the kind of customer we want to attract.

The best marketing has a heartbeat, a humanity, and I would argue that when that heartbeat and humanity come from the top of the business, that is where the best kind of success comes from. People want to connect with other humans. We are neurologically wired for connection. So let your customers connect with you, even if the ways you want to create that connection feel crazy or too big or too scary.

The best ideas I have ever had, the biggest projects I have ever done, the concepts that have allowed my business to grow, were all born of something that felt crazy, required me to be my authentic self, or an out-of-left field idea that I believed in immensely. Let me give you some examples of what I mean.

When I got in a rut with my boudoir bookings in 2017 (*boudoir*, for those of you who don't know, are sexy, empowering photo shoots that center on creating intimate images that celebrate yourself! They are most often seen as something for women to do but I believe in the power of boudoir for everyone!), one of the first ideas that popped into my head was to create an event where babes could come and see what a boudoir session with me was like in a fun, party environment. Boudoir feels a little scary for clients because it's vulnerable, but I believed if folks could see how fun it was, the fear would subside, and my bookings would increase.

I had this idea on a Tuesday and four days later, my first Self Love Saturday was born. I hastily threw together this totally free event and twenty-six babes showed up wearing things that made them feel like the most empowered version of themselves. I shot each person for two to three minutes, walked the group through what a full session can look like, and while this became an annual event that definitely got better with each year, that first event is near and dear to my heart.

I didn't wait for it to be perfect though. It was a late night, crazy idea that I just went for, figuring it was either going to be a waste of a Saturday afternoon with folks getting free photos, or it would do what I needed, which was to fill my calendar with more clients. And it worked!

Those folks shared their photos and told their friends which resulted in twenty-eight new bookings as a result of that first Self Love Saturday. My next one the following year looked different and the one after that grew upon the lessons from the first two. And in the three years since, this event alone has grossed over $95,000 and allowed me to fill my calendar with clients who are really excited to work with me and share in my idea that loving, seeing, and showing up for yourself at a photoshoot can really change your life.

But when I had shared this idea with industry friends before doing it, none of them believed it could have that kind of success. To them, doing something for free was a bad idea; it was too much work for no promised reward and how in the world would I pull it off in such a short time frame? I believed in the idea though; I believed in myself, and I am so glad I did.

I also found this in the willingness to live as my authentic, openly queer self. I never fully came out until I started dating my now wife eight years ago. I did my best to walk this fine line of not being "too queer" but also not ever being myself. I feared that in coming out as a business, I would lose much of the original client base I had and that was a valid fear that did, in fact, come true.

You see, most of my original clients came from the Christian college I went to and church connections I had, so coming out meant that most of those folks no longer wanted to support me or my business. It meant losing a relationship with my parents, and with almost every childhood friend. And it was hard. I could write a whole other chapter on how that was for me but for the sake of time, I'll go with *hard*.

On the other side of that though, was this beautiful photography family that I would create. At the time gay marriage had just been legalized nationwide and living openly as a queer person was risky and many folks said it might be better to just keep that part of myself from the public eye. But coming out as a business has allowed me to not only work with clients who are like me but also, it's given me access to telling stories I might not otherwise have been able to.

And from a financial perspective? I can trace where my company became profitable to when I finally fully came out as a business. Since coming out as a business in 2014, I have worked with over 250 LGBTQ+ couples and brought in over $500,000 in income from their weddings alone. I have made my website a safe and celebratory space for not only LGBTQ+ folks but also for folks with larger bodies or different styles of expression. Being all about everyone and celebrating all love and bodies and stories equally wasn't something that I saw modeled growing up or in business circles, but it has been not only a financial win but brought so much joy to my life as well.

Those ideas all came from a place of story, of connectedness, of daring to do something that others might call crazy. They also came from my being willing to do something, often something free, that resonated with my "Why" as a business owner. They have allowed my business to grow in ways I never imagined, and I am deeply grateful that I made the choice to choose myself, my ideas, and my vision of success over what others *might* think or suggest I do.

All those stories as a child, all those books that showed me what it meant to live in my own authenticity prepared me to be a business owner that wants the same. And so, my call to you isn't to disregard everything you might have read in a book or heard from talented business owners, but to instead learn and listen, then trust the daring, crazy ideas you have inside you. Be brave enough to do the things you believe in but might be alone in doing.

What's the worst that can happen? You waste some time on something that resonates with you? You are out some money on an idea that didn't work? The end result is a flop? Or maybe, instead, your wild idea brings you new clients, your shift back to your own authenticity resonates with the clients, your clear "Why" brings you customers that are excited to buy from you. There is no way to know without trying.

I believe that this world doesn't need more businesses doing the same things that have been successful in the past, but rather businesses who dare to rewrite the script, embrace their own ideas, and use connection as a way to bring what you do or sell to others. You are your business's greatest asset and your stories, your ideas, your crazy vision is ultimately what it needs to **thrive**.

AMANDA SWIGER

Amanda Swiger is a visionary that feels called to create space for folks to feel seen as their authentic selves. She is also a multi-genre, award-winning photographer who loves bold color, laughter, and folks madly in love with themselves and/or their partner. She resides outside Philadelphia, PA with her wife and rescue dog Furgie.

Website: www.swigerphotography.com   .
Instagram: @swigerphotography or @philadelphiaboudoir

11

REFRAMING DOUBT

The dictionary defines *marginalized* as, "to put or keep (someone) in a powerless or unimportant position within a society or group." When I think about this word, it feels like the energy of the sun encompasses my entire body with nowhere to hide the intensity. I'm experiencing "stuckness" with needing to accept my fate. Existing in this template tends to tighten the lid on recognizing our own strengths through doubt.

Doubt has been spilling into my brain for decades - taking many forms, shapes, sizes + impacts. As part of the LGBTQ+ community, we've all had limiting beliefs instilled. I've heard and internalized my fair share—these are mine:

> *You are not deserving of this opportunity*
> *You are not valued*
> *You don't deserve to get paid equal to your cis-het*
>   *counterparts*
> *You don't deserve to be acknowledged*
> *Your thoughts are not good enough*
> *Your neurodivergence does not belong here*

You're short
You're fat
You're too dark AND you're too light

You aren't trans
You aren't queer enough

Does this sound familiar? If so, I hold compassion for you as you continue to consume these words. These words create deep wounds and I hope this chapter allows for some healing.

So, let's talk about it. Doubt is continuously reinforced from person to person at the speed of our own thoughts.

Let's imagine a domino effect; you're placing each domino in hopes that once the first domino is down, the rest go down with it. Each domino can represent a seed of doubt planted into our brains beginning at a young age. One of my earliest memories was playing tag in elementary school with the boys and being told "You are never going to be as good as us because you're a girl."

Two things came up here: the seed of doubt that I'm never going to be as good as boys at physical activities and that I am + can only be a girl, which will forever make me less than. Talk about planting seeds! I wish six-year-old Noopur was able to articulate this, rather it was learned by twenty-six-year-old Noopur.

DURING THE PANDEMIC there has been an immense amount of introspection required for my emotional survival. When we are under the confines of capitalism we tend to move fast—faster than we are meant to move around the world doing all we do daily. Then March 2020 comes around and the world shuts down.

As I questioned my own value without acknowledgement, I began to view our capitalistic system with significant skepticism and resistance. This happened in ways that I could have never imagined.

You know that feeling of starting a new job right out of school? You are doe-eyed, ready to conquer everything ahead of you! That was me in 2019. I graduated with my master's in counseling and was quickly offered a job from a then-trusted professor and supervisor. My blinders were on, I was never able to recognize from where my self-doubt stemmed.

But then came quarantine. Lock down. Shut down. Whatever you called it, it was fucking happening. Everything began changing at alarming rates. I began seeing clients virtually and we would just talk about the pandemic, specifically the unknowns around it. We began to experience the impacts of working from home and/or being required to go to a physical work setting in the midst of a deadly pandemic. I lived and began working in a 600 sq/ft apartment with my wife and two cats.

This small space left me with little room to exhale and opened up never-ending room for introspection. Seeds of doubt and gaslighting were being placed throughout the pandemic, impacting marginalized groups of people the most. My seeds of doubt flared up significantly. The difference was the slow down, the pause, the requirement to sit with yourself because you are not going out into the world doing the things you would "normally" do.

In August 2020, I found myself miserable. At this point I was stuck in a job that did not see me as a person, rather as a trans brown face on a website. I did not realize that this was occurring until I was completely dismissed several times when expressing difficulty and/or requesting help. I found myself asking for help less and less but then feeling more burnout; in hindsight, it makes so much sense.

I am a fiery person, I'm an Aries. I'm extroverted, passionate, and tend to take up more space than others. The fact that I was feeling defeated, sad, stuck, and shameful was a bit new. This was the sign.

Our bodies offer signals; this one was "something is wrong, and this should not be happening." In this moment I needed to listen to the doubt without letting it consume me. I chose to listen to the doubt that my intuition was offering me without judgment. Of course, this did not happen overnight, but with support in other facets of my life, I was able to begin recognizing the ways I was being harmed in a white cis-led system that continued to consistently place doubt onto me.

I remember one specific supervision session where my supervisor asked me how I was doing. Now, this was June of last year, pretty soon after George Floyd's murder. I felt deeply impacted and was having some difficulty maintaining the caseload that I had at the time without processing what I was experiencing. So, having this question asked felt like being given permission to process this out loud with someone.

I told them how I was experiencing the pandemic and the murder of George Floyd, and their response was jarring to my expression of vulnerability. "How can you use what you're experiencing for your clients?" This generally is a great question! But something was confirmed to me at that moment. I am just an appliance + placeholder to these white people. The blatant disregard to my human experience crushed me.

This was the last straw for me, but there were several ways doubt was reinforced in the workplace:

- Continually having my abilities questioned without constructive feedback or reasoning for questioning me
- Denied creativity by being told no most times I offered an idea that would benefit the practice + clients
- Being empowered to put myself out there + network within community without any mat to fall on felt like I was being set up for failure

I remember leaving the job late last year and being questioned about my decision-making skills prior to my last day. "Are you sure you don't want to stay here? Do you feel like that's a good idea for your finances? We have health insurance, sounds like your other job doesn't." They wanted me to be a complicit queer brown puzzle piece to their big white picture. Something to remember: your light + growth is going to bother unhealed people. It is inherent for humans to feel jealousy and project onto others.

Capitalism impacts the confidence of those who seemingly "step out of line." When navigating structures that don't have queer folks in mind, we run into barriers: physical and emotional. It all starts before we even get here.

Our parents find out that they are about to have a baby and their entire idea of who we will become begins to form. Investing in gender norms begins from a gender reveal party, continues through reinforcing colors with gender, along with the clothes you are "allowed" and "not allowed" to wear, and finally, the careers you are supposed to pursue.

Gender and capitalism are intertwined: If you really think about it, everything we purchase has an expectation stamp on top of it. Being in the LGBTQ+ community is definitely opposing the expectation stamp. I was wearing masculine clothing when I was just a kiddo and because that did not fit the expectation for me at the time, I was labeled a "tomboy." This, in retrospect, really was code for "my child is challenging gender roles and the binary but we can't really say anything."

As queer folks, our avenue to success requires these three things: networking within community, personal boundary setting + deepening our relationship with ourselves. Our barriers to reaching the end are more intricate, more difficult, and have more room for disaster as we attempt to build and just be. As you are picking out the barriers to your success, you are hypervigilant, you are in survival mode, you are anticipating the worst but hoping for the best. Feels like tightness. Trying to detach tangled barbed wire. This can feel unknown, unfamiliar, and painful. Over time we become less connected to ourselves and continue to rely on others to reassure + validate our worth.

Three Tools to Conquer LGBTQ+ Self-Doubt

Networking

BEING BELIEVED in by someone else and accepting this form of care can be really uncomfortable. It can be difficult to allow that perception in, but it is important for your greatness to be reinforced. It starts with networking within the LGBTQ+/Queer community.

The goal is to connect with those who believe in you and do not plant seeds of doubt. Find the right people and give yourself permission to thrive. Put yourself out there in order to understand that your experience is not unique, and you deserve empowerment. You might not like it sometimes, but you need to listen to those who offer empowerment and compassion and validate your experiences, people that push you rather than coddle you/keep you comfy. Sometimes folks keeping you comfortable are hoping to keep you complacent.

I watched a documentary where T-Pain opened up about the doubt that was implanted when he started becoming successful. He was on a plane with some prominent figures in music and one who he considered to be his closest friend said to him, "You know, you ruined music" because he was one of the first to popularize Auto-Tune.

This planted the seeds of doubt that grew into long-term depression which resulted in him never pursuing the dreams that were bigger. Fast forward to the *Masked Singer* finale of season one. There was a character called the Monster who was spectacular in every single episode and left people in awe because of how beautiful and talented their voice was. Monster finally takes off his mask and the world sees T-Pain, someone who had only ever been known for auto tune and "ruining music." He was one of the first artists who was honest in his use of Auto-Tune.

This shed some perspective on me as I thought about my own experiences as the first out queer + trans person in my family, the first to get their degree in the mental health field and the first to cut their hair, + get tattoos within the family. I remember feeling that I ruined the family expectation + honor through how I was treated as I navigated new waters.

Representation in the workplace is great, but protection allows for sustainability and real change. A lack of representation and protection (safety and support) can quickly manifest into burnout. As an individual holding several identities that are less represented and struggling with this reality prior to considering myself, it is crucial to begin being curious of your own physical and emotional boundaries/needs.

Boundary Setting

Doubt helps you learn about yourself (what you're needing and NOT needing) and can begin the conversation around boundaries for yourself. Boundary setting with others is great, but I'm going to encourage you to be a little selfish here. What boundaries are for you and just you? This requires a heightened consideration of yourself.

One way to explore your personal boundaries is through identifying what has not worked in the past. For example, I recognized that I need feedback from my supervisor, so I requested + expected those needs to be met. We need to lift as we climb.

Another way to explore this is through a pros and cons list. Asking questions like: What is serving me? What is detrimental and negatively impacting me? This allows your perspective to expand and explore beyond the tunnel vision that has been created through doubt.

Deepen your Relationship with Yourself

Doubt shows you where you are not free. Your brain soaks up the one seed of doubt and is watered through reinforcement of doubt + believing you deserve that treatment. A metaphor that encompasses this idea is "it only takes a teaspoon of crude oil to ruin a submarine's entire water supply."

Beginning to deepen your self-understanding takes time, patience, and self-compassion. Remember, this growth + healing adventure is not linear. It will feel wavy, joyous at some points, devastating at others. You do not deserve the suffering you've experienced; all these lessons were possible without that suffering. Maybe it is time to slow down and give yourself a chance even if it feels uncomfortable. Discomfort when doing something for yourself tends to be a good thing.

I was with a buddy who gave me a tarot reading while working on this chapter and The Hierophant pulled my energy. Representing joy through exhaustion, feeling grounded and ready. This card has pink, bright, vibrant tones with the most joyous human sitting in front of a golden stairwell.

I saw that and was mesmerized, let me tell you! All I wanted to do was climb up the golden stairwell, but then I paused. I've been climbing that golden stairwell for quite some time now. You have and are doing this too.

I am now working for a community practice that values each individual as a piece of the healing puzzle. The growth is now built from empowerment, trust, support, and love. This is now trickling into the clients and people who I work with. I am holding compassion + space for each and every one of you who are struggling and working through this to obtain whatever it is you are needing.

NOOPUR SHAH

(THEY/HE), FIRST GEN. INDIAN / TRANS NB / CLINICAL THERAPIST

My passion happens to be being curious about others to build a deep understanding of their experience and have compassion throughout. I have over three years of experience as a clinical therapist, currently primarily working with trans + gender diverse children, adolescents + adults to empower them in their identities. I am a first generation South Asian, trans/gender diverse, neuro-divergent individual. As a child of immigrants, there was a cultural expectation of prioritizing others' needs before my own –

over time I began building autonomy through my own therapeutic experiences. This allowed me to approach myself with more understanding, allowing me to explore my gender identity. My creativity in my work is fueled by holding emotional space for others + cultivating community through creating and running therapeutic groups. When I'm not working, I am spending time with loved ones (my wife, cats, family, and friends), weightlifting with other queer folks, and being goofy.

Website: forrealtherapy.com/noopur-shah
Instagram: @queerindiantherapist

12

PITCHING WITH AUTHENTICITY, CLARITY, AND STYLE

As an entrepreneur, you will find yourself constantly pitching. Whether it's a formal pitch at a StartOut Demo Day, an initial meeting with prospective investors at Starbucks, or recruiting your first engineer… you will continually be sharing about your venture and your vision seeking others to fund, join, promote, or buy.

I recognize that many of us shy away from being too "self-promotional," but to succeed, you will need to overcome whatever inner voices may tell you to "tone it down." While pitching itself is not that different for LGBTQIA+ individuals and our non-gay (or straight) counterparts, many of us begin at a disadvantage because of messages we've heard and internalized about our own identity, expression, or orientation.

Let me say it right up front: You are worthy to start this business and seek this funding! If you feel you are not, then work with a mentor to dispel those voices. My own inner critic has been with me for decades and still creeps into my psyche. Now (in my mid 50s) I acknowledge these voices as "old acquaintances" who show up uninvited. They should take a seat and not be heard from while I'm pitching. I don't try to fight these voices, nor do I give them any space in my head to divert me.

The place I urge you to start is from authenticity. Don't try to be something you're not... investors will sniff that out quickly. Be yourself, be confident, and be connected. Everything you say or do communicates something to somebody somehow. Own what you are projecting and presenting as an authentic representation of who you are and what you have to say and ask of others.

Through our authentic presence we author the reputation by which we wish to be known. Several entrepreneurs who provided me input for this chapter urged me to expand authenticity to include vulnerability (not weakness mind you). When we embody these qualities fully, we are compelling to others. With that authentic and confident self in place, let me suggest what you should do before, during, and after a pitch (any conversation where you share your idea and seek support... be it financial or otherwise.)

Before: Establish your AIM and do your Research

If you've ever sat in a workshop or class I've taught, you know where I almost always begin: AIM (Audience, Intent, and Message). This model, developed by Lynn Russell and Mary Munter, (*Guide to Presentations*, 2014) is both simple and clear and should be used by any entrepreneur before launching into any communication (written or spoken). Ask yourself these three questions (in this order!):

1. Who is my **audience?**
2. What is my **intent?**
3. What is my **message?**

You cannot move to messaging until you are clear on who you are addressing and what you hope to accomplish. Pull out all the stops as you research the people you will be meeting. Certainly, start with LinkedIn, but go further. See if you can clearly establish their tie to the LGBTQIA+ community (as a member or strong ally) and to your specific venture. As one entrepreneur shared with me, "as part of a small community of people, there's often a natural affinity to want to help each other. Being out won't get you an investor, but it might get you in the door." Another emphasized, "Being out didn't help or hurt me, but you have to have passion and a clear compelling idea that will provide a return on their investment."

The more that you can build your own gay/queer network the better. Register for conferences (there's likely twenty different "out" events each year), join organizations, and attend benefits in our community. The more you are out and about (pun fully intended) the more you can build and maintain a strong network.

Even if you were not out while in college (or high school) it's worth exploring if your alma mater has any sort of pride group for alumni. If you can connect naturally with others in our world, you will foster the network you need when you have specific requests to make. This part of the process can be fun; it's like sleuthing (not stalking) to see if you can create a portrait of the person before you meet. If you've been invited, introduced, or scheduled by another (whom I will call the gatekeeper), rely on that person for all the information you can so that you will succeed. Try to determine "Why would *this* person invest in *this* idea?"

Be audience-centric in your preparation. When you consider your intent, remember it's not what you want, it's what you want THEM to think, say, or do. Intent exists in the hearts and minds of the receiver. Create an active phrase starting with a verb that captures your intent. You want the other person to **invest** in your venture, **introduce** you to somebody, **critique** your idea, **agree** to a longer meeting, etc. Consider, too, that intents are not just about the money; sometimes the best gift you can receive is candid feedback about your venture, or a crucial introduction to the right person to advise you.

During: Develop Rapport while Delivering Clear Content

Now that you've done your prep and have a meeting scheduled, it's time to step into the pitch and succeed. Deliver a compelling message so this audience will take the action you intend. You have two complementary tasks at this stage: build rapport and deliver your content. Each pitch is a conversation, and you may have to flexibly move between these two tasks throughout.

At its core, pitching is relational not transactional. Listen intently to what they share, pose open-ended questions to get to know them and their interests better, and be genuinely curious about the other person.

I've explored many books that espouse "the right way" to pitch, but of the entire field I have one that has worked best for me and the founders I've coached: Chris Lipp's four-point model from his book *The Startup Pitch: A Proven Formula to Win Funding* (2014). Chris reverse-engineered his model by analyzing the winners of TechCrunch over a three-year period. He found that over 90 percent of those funded followed this intuitive formula:

- Problem – proving that a problem exists which demands solution
- Solution – tying your innovation to the problem and showing your impact
- Market – detailing that people (or entities) are willing to pay for this solution
- Business – demonstrating that you've built a business model to capture this revenue

As you develop (or adjust) your pitch, I strongly urge you to check out Lipp's book and the resources on his site, pitchpower.org. He's generously allowed me to detail this in my own book, *Communicate with Mastery* (2020), too, in chapter four.

The key to his model is that you need to cover all four

elements, in that order. You cannot skip over a stage, but you can decide how much time/attention you give to it. If the problem is pretty evident to most people in your audience, that portion may be brief... but not assumed and eliminated.

Within the pitch don't be annoyed or distracted by questions, see these as fantastic! It means the person is listening and engaging. You are much better off delivering 40 percent of what you planned but having addressed their questions and met their needs than to have gotten through 100 percent of your pitch, with no signal as to how interested the investor may be.

My friend, David Hornik of Lobby Capital, shared that "Most of the real work gets done in the questions. They are your chance to demonstrate knowledge, thoughtfulness, and preparedness. Don't discourage questions, encourage them. If you can engage investors in a conversation, you are more likely to not only develop a relationship, but also demonstrate your skills as an entrepreneur."

At times you may choose to pitch with one or more other members of your team. When you choose to do this, recognize that it's a choice (like most in life) with clear payoffs and drawbacks. The benefit is that it allows you to show greater diversity on your team, demonstrate your ability to collaborate, and have an extra set of eyes in the pitch to keep it on track. Further, a colleague in the room with you can gauge reactions for you: Where were they amused, confused, or annoyed? What resonated most?

But before you rush to bring all the founders to every pitch, keep in mind the inherent risks. First, it's much harder to keep two or more speakers on time. This can create tension among the team that can signal disunity to the prospective investors. Additionally, while diversity is great, different styles may be hard to integrate without time invested in rehearsal. Finally, it's very easy for one person to dominate the pitch, which can then show poorly to the investor and irritate the hell out of your peers.

Finally, within the pitch, it's great if you can synthesize and write down next steps as the conversation draws to a close. Note what promises you (and your team) have made and by when you can make good on this. Ideally that will cue the other person to tick through their list too. If not, then gently offer what you recall they promised. If a follow-up meeting is warranted, see if you can get them to commit to the meeting now, or clear the way for you to work with somebody who can schedule it. Don't lose the momentum by an endless volley of emails back and forth trying to set the time and day of the next meeting.

After: Your Success in Follow-through can Seal the Deal

I look at this in concentric circles of time after the meeting:

Within minutes – stop and capture what happened. Put all new contacts into your CRM (or snap a photo for another person to input for you) and put all your promises directly into your calendar. Most crucially, in a handwritten journal, capture what you learned and what you can change in future pitches. This very quick "postmortem" can be done with others who were in the pitch, even if they didn't speak. My whole approach to communication mastery is centered on "incremental improvement" in everything we write or speak.

Within 24 hours – acknowledge and thank them. This can be a quick email or text (if that's appropriate for the person) or a quick handwritten note (my favorite, but that's likely a generational bias.) Don't use this to ask for anything or remind them of their promises, simply and genuinely thank them for their time, insight, and experience. If you picked up on something of shared interest, follow up with a tip or reference. I love to share TED talks with people afterwards who I think may enjoy them, while my best friend Javier usually follows up with restaurants they should explore. Again, keep it brief, authentic, and related.

Within an appropriate (and established) time frame – meet all the other promises you made, and then move the prospective investor to the logical next step. Ideally that's from inquiry to prospect to trial user to customer, etc. but sometimes it's not that linear. What you do want to avoid is letting somebody languish in "waiting for a response" land. If they have interest, build on the momentum, and get the next meeting in place. And, if they don't have interest, let them go. Agree to not keep pestering a "no" or annoying a "maybe." You need to spend time with people willing to invest time, money, and resources in you. Within what's appropriate, gently nudge them to move forward or graciously allow them to part ways. It's in their interest and yours to not just languish.

It's unfortunate but many people will not tell you "No" directly. They may say "Not now" or "Let's stay connected" but not free you up to move on with a clear statement. As you have press announcements or product launches it may be a perfect time to re-engage prospective investors by keeping them posted on your progress.

Synthesis: It's about Relationships not Transactions

You want to approach the pitch as just one specific element of a longer term, more nuanced, and more complex relationship. Invariably you will encounter the same individuals again and again through your life as an entrepreneur. Build a reputation as somebody who prioritizes relationships over transactions and honors their promises to others. If you can do that with authenticity, clarity, and a sense of personal style, you will go far. Pitching effectively can provide you the resources you need to find success as an LGBTQIA+ entrepreneur. Working for yourself and building an entity that employs others and creates value in the world is one of the greatest callings I know. Make the most of it.

JD SCHRAMM

JD Schramm, EdD, is the author of *Communicate with Mastery: Speak with Conviction and Write for Impact.* An entrepreneur since age eight he's also coached other entrepreneurs to be successful for over twenty-five years. His 2011 TED talk, *Break the Silence for Suicide Attempt Survivors,* has over two million views and his forthcoming book, *The Bridge Back to Life: My Journey from the Edge of Death to the Center of Life,* examines the steps he took in his own recovery process from depression and addiction. He and his husband, Rev.

Ken Daigle, have three children and live in Marin County, just outside San Francisco.

Website: jdschramm.com
Email: jd@jdschramm.com
LinkedIn: https://www.linkedin.com/in/jdschramm/

13

FINDING THE REAL YOU

I have the best job in the entire world. I find gratitude every day for all the decisions I made that got me here. But believe me, I didn't always love my job—hell, I didn't always love myself. Being human isn't all rainbows and butterflies. So, in order to tell you how I got here, I have to tell you a bit about where I came from.

In my journey to self-discovery, there was one night I remember specifically. *It was a horrible night.* I remember looking in the mirror and not recognizing the person staring back at me.

Actually, actually... hold on... let me back up and be honest... because I was totally drunk staring at myself in this mirror... And that was probably the twentieth night in a row I was looking into the bloodshot eyes of a stranger.

I had just gotten out of a toxic relationship.

I lost my job.

I was the unhealthiest I had ever been.

I had no drive or passion anymore.

I felt like I was running on fumes, but I realized I wasn't just running on E. No... I was just running. I was running from what my life could have been if I could just get completely honest with myself. If I could stop hanging onto all the stories I told myself as a kid that became my beliefs about what I was capable of as an adult, I could rest; I could stop running.

Things like...

You're taking up so much space.

You're "too" gay.

No one will listen to you.

No one will like you.

Believing all those stories kept me stagnant. And let me tell you—when you're staring into the unknown, it's really fucking easy to want to turn around and run towards the familiar; towards what's safe, even if it's self-destructive. But I knew in order to get the life I never had, I needed to do things I had never done before. Status quo just wasn't working.

So, instead of staying comfortable, I turned, and I didn't walk into the unknown—I ran. I ran towards things I had never done before even though my heart was racing.

Ever since starting my company, Only Human, I've been labeled as an "influencer" by a lot of people. But I'm no influencer.

I'm just a human who decided that my rock bottom didn't have to be where I unpacked and lived. So, I'm not going to tell you how to build a huge following, create a brand, or how to build your online image. **In this chapter, I'm going to talk about how you find yourself and then you find the people who know and support the real you.**

When I started this journey, I didn't have the 100k followers in a global community like we do now. This was never about creating some online brand. It was about sharing my story and listening to other people share theirs. I never could have imagined that sharing my growth journey would lead to life-altering conversations, new ways to create an impact, and building a platform that doesn't just sell clothes—but saves lives.

As a kid, I couldn't have dreamt as big as my life has become until I got out of my own way. These three steps helped me get out of my own way; I hope they can do the same for you.

Step 1: Is what you're consuming, consuming you?

Too often we think about consumption in terms of what we put into our bodies. Don't get me wrong, paying attention to what I was eating and drinking was necessary for my physical health, but **the biggest shift I had for my mental health came when I started focusing on the content I was consuming.** The shitty TV shows I was binge watching, the books I wasn't reading, the social media accounts I was comparing myself to, in the end, all of it was keeping me small.

When I got honest about consumption it didn't just change what I was eating and drinking…. I changed what I was reading, listening to, and watching.

That small habit shift quickly changed all the people I surrounded myself with. **Because lemme tell you, recognizing the number of people in my life who were just "happy hour friends" was startling.**

And that awakening became the platform to the next change I needed to make. Because that night looking into the eyes in the mirror, I couldn't see clearly. So, it was time to refocus. Step two was all about finding clarity.

Step 2: Do you know what you want from your life?

How OFTEN DO you sit and reflect on what it is you truly value in life? If I asked you, right now, to name the top five things you value in life, friendships, and relationships, could you do it?

In the beginning of my reflection process I thought I valued things like success, merit, or perfection. I realized quickly that those things were what I thought I should value. It's what my teachers instilled in me; it's what I heard laced in every sentence as they told me I had to get into a good college.

I started reading books like *Start With Why* by Simon Sinek, *The Gifts Of Imperfection* by Brene Brown, *The Four Agreements* by Don Miguel Ruiz, and *What I Know For Sure* by Oprah.

Throwing myself into learning new ways of thinking and unthinking sent me on a new reflective journey. Soon my journal was full of pages and pages of mind maps, tear-stained entries, and reflections on what I cared about most. Suddenly, I became more and more aware of my own voice in my head, and less in-tune with society's thoughts on how I was meant to live a fulfilled life.

Below are thirteen journal prompts that helped me discover what matters the most to me. I recommend taking space and a physical pen and paper to write about these. When you're done reflecting on each, choose three answers to each question and keep them short and sweet (one to three words). After you're done, take all thirty-nine answers and start to group them into similar categories. This will help you start to identify the things you invest your time, money, and energy into.

1. How do you fill the spaces you occupy?
2. What are the top three things you spend your awake time doing?
3. Where do you put your energy? What energizes you the most?
4. What do you spend your money on?
5. Where in your life are you the most organized?
6. Where are you the most disciplined and reliable?
7. What do you think about most?
8. What do you talk to others about the most?
9. What do you talk to yourself about the most?
10. What do you talk to others about the most?
11. What inspires you the most?
12. What are your long-term goals that are coming true?
13. What do you love to learn about the most?

IT TOOK me years of reflection, self-work, and vulnerable conversations with myself and others to find my core values. This is no easy task, so take your time and be gentle on yourself. Growth is not easy, but I promise you, inauthenticity will be harder.

MY TOP FIVE VALUES:

1. Self-growth
2. Technology
3. Community
4. Creativity
5. Habits

When I started getting really clear on what it was that mattered to me, I started to notice that the places and people I was putting myself around weren't in alignment with what I knew in my heart I wanted my life to be. It became more and more clear that it wasn't that life wasn't "going my way," it was that I wasn't even walking in the right direction.

I recognized that I needed to start putting myself in new situations and around new people in order to figure out what it was that would support my vision and align with my values. One of my favorite quotes kept ringing in my head...

"You know, sometimes all you need is twenty seconds of insane courage. Just literally twenty seconds of just embarrassing bravery. And I promise you, something great will come of it." - Benjamin Mee, *We Bought A Zoo*

So, I started building vision boards full of pictures and quotes that supported what I actually wanted in my life, and I looked at it every day. I started scary conversations with strangers that I looked up to hoping to hear their recipe for success. I attended coaching workshops, met with mentors at countless coffee shops, and did things that made me nervous and pushed me out of my comfort zone.

So, then, when people kept coming to me, wanting to know how I did it, how I found myself and my people, I could tell them it's because I stopped putting myself in spaces that didn't feel good, and I started doing the things I had been too afraid to do. I put myself in spaces that gave me the chance—the opportunity—to meet people who valued what I valued.

Step 3: Who are you surrounding yourself with?

YOU SEE, when you know who you are, people have the chance to get to know that person. And the only way to find people who like the real you is to *be* **the real you.**

For so long, I had been what I thought everyone else wanted me to be. I had molded myself into the person that made others feel comfortable at my own sacrifice. I had kept my mouth shut about the things that mattered to me all because the people around me didn't feel comfortable with talking about the hard shit. Doing that for so long made me feel like a hollow shell. And that night, looking in the mirror—that's exactly what I saw.

So, when I got honest about that, when I could own that the only person who was going to change my life was me, **I could start taking action.**

Anyone has the power to cultivate an entirely new life. But it's going to mean getting vulnerable. And the first person you gotta open up to—is yourself. It means getting honest about what it is you're holding yourself back from. It means sitting with yourself... maybe even being lonely at times, because in that space, you meet the real you. Once I met the real me, I decided that the biggest bet I wanted to make in life was on myself and my own ability to turn my pain into purpose.

And so, Only Human (onlyhumanco.com) was born. It was a thing I created to find myself and a community to support me. It was born from my hard times, from my growth, and it was created at my rock bottom knowing that if I needed it, so would others.

Since starting Only Human in 2016 I've traveled all over the world meeting humans who might look different than me, but still need and want for the same things. Things like love, support, honesty, and the chance to share who they are with others and not be judged for their journey.

Only Human was built to house the stories of the broken and the beautiful. It was built to share resources, connect with others, and give back to our communities... together.

Each month we partner with a new non-profit and run what we call a Cause Campaign where we design a line of positive-message apparel and donate 10% of sales; we have an online community of over 6,000 Advocates in over forty countries; we share stories of humans impacted by the cause; we hold events and Q&A spaces to learn and grow; we volunteer in local communities.

Every single day I ~~have~~ *get* to wake up and do work that not only fills my soul, but truly aligns with it. The work I do at OH fosters self-growth on an individual and group level, is driven by technology and social ties, brings together communities to give back, allows me to be creative, and creates space in my life for the habits that keep me in balance.

So now when I check in with my values, I can clearly see them at play in my everyday personal and professional life. It's what makes work feel more like passion. It's allowed me to create an income with an impact, which to me is the deepest form of wealth I could ever have. But remember...

Growing might feel like breaking at first, but sometimes the healing IS the aching.

All I can hope for you is that you feel inspired to open up, to look in your own mirror, and reflect on who you are and what matters the most to you. When you begin to do that, you won't need to find your people. **Your people will find you.**

BREE PEAR

Meet Bree. She's a tech-nerd entrepreneur with a passion for humans and a drive to make waves in this world. In 2016 Bree founded Only Human—a platform for good that brings humans together for a deeper purpose. After hitting rock bottom in her own life, she recognized that she had the power to change her narrative and use her skills to help bring others together. Bree truly believes that by building a community of like-minded humans willing to make changes in this world, we can create a ripple effect that's felt on a global scale.

Website: https://hoo.be/onlyhuman
Instagram: https://instagram.com/breepear
Email: Bree@onlyhumanco.com

14

THE AUDACITY TO THINK BIGGER

Baby entrepreneurs,
  Have the audacity to think bigger.
  Forget what your parents, partners, and society told you. You can have whatever it is you want in this life. You have full permission to chase your desires and build a reality of your very own.

It may feel selfish or arrogant at first, but in truth, your happiness needs to come first, always. When you're happy, you are at your best; when you are at your best, you're showing up for others at full capacity.

You were born for more and we're going to work together to help you believe it.

Dream a little with me.

What desires have you never dared to speak about out loud?

What are your audacious, scare-the-crap-out-of-you goals? What's been in the backseat of your mind?

It could be flying first class from Chicago to Tokyo.

It could be living out of a van and driving across the country.

Whatever it is, it's 1000% possible for you to achieve and I want to help you feel good and deserving of those goals.

Nothing is out of reach.

Here's the secret sauce:

I'm gonna share with you an exercise that I learned in my own coaching program through JRNI life coach training (slightly modified for this text). **It's called the 5D cycle.**

Define

Discover

Dream

Design

and Destiny

Grab your notebook and a pen, it's about to get good! As we walk through each portion of this exercise, I want you to give yourself permission to be a kid again. What was it that you wanted and who were you before the world told you what was "allowed"?

Define

Starting from the top, write out and define what a luxurious and glamorous life looks like for **you.** For some, it may look like having a certain dollar amount in their checking account. For others, it may simply mean taking vacations a few times per year. Getting super specific on your definition of success is the most crucial part of this process.

What experiences, possessions, or status would make you stop and say, "I made it"?

Take your time with this, marinate in it! Dream it up!

Discover

Now time to explore a little! Think back to all of the times in your life you have *already* experienced some of what you defined.

For example, if you wrote that you want more career success, think back to all the wins you've had so far. Nothing is too small. Remember your first client? Maybe you brought on another team member or sold a new offer. There are a thousand moments in your past where you've already experienced at least a sliver of what you desire more of. Write them down and soak in them!

Now dig a little deeper. I want you to write down what you value most about yourself, your relationships, and your work.

This is not the time to be humble. Nothing is too minimal.

Who are you when you are at 100 percent, all pistons firing?

How do you show up?

Who do you impact by showing up in this way?

How does it feel to be able to show up so fully?

Don't rush through this. Take your time. Sit with any feelings that come up and take note.

Dream

Now that you've soaked in your exceptionalism, let's get a little wild. It's time to build a roadmap from where we are to where we want to go. This is the portion of the process where we get to laser focus on what we want for ourselves and how past positive experiences can be inflated to become our wildest dreams.

This phase is all about looking at your dreams, knowing they are achievable, and then taking the dreams one step further. Whatever it is you had in mind, add to it… amplify it. Multiply it by ten.

Here is an example. One of my dreams is to write a book that helps people. So let's take that one step further - I am going to write a *New York Times* best seller and get an invitation to speak at a TedX conference.

Does my dream sound audacious? I hope so. That's the point!

In truth, I'm a living testament to this 5D process. I am at the very beginning of my business journey and this chapter is one of my first publications geared towards helping queer entrepreneurs accumulate wealth.

I'm early on in my journey but I know where I'm going, and I have a clear path on how I want to get there.

Design

This is where the rubber meets the road. It's time to outline actionable steps to make your dreams a reality.

I want you to look at your life and look at what might need to shift in your world so it better aligns with your dream.

- What habits do you have?
- What are your processes and systems?
- What roles are you taking on in your life?
- What are your resources and what resources do you need to accumulate?
- What relationships, connections, and mentors do you have? What new connections need to be made?
- What do your finances look like right now? Where do you want them to be and how are you going to get there?
- If you don't know how to get to the places that you want to be, who can you talk to and who can you hire if need be?
- What structures are currently in place to enable you to continuously move forward toward your dreams?

It's important to get as detailed and as personal as possible. We need the details to inform actionable steps and feed progress toward your goals. It's important to get really intimate with your ambitions, make it personal. When it's personal, there is some more skin in the game and feeling connected to your plan will help you feel connected to your dreams.

Destiny

This phase is not something that will just fall in your lap as the title implies. You are in charge of your own destiny and must take the action steps outlined in Design for this to work.

You cannot be stagnant.

Destiny is all about continuously finding your purpose in your plan and absorbing the steps as if through osmosis. You are a sponge for your dreams. All you need to do is boldly work through your plan and soak up the opportunities as they come.

A final word before you go:

Let's chat a little about what we were taught growing up.

You've been told that money is a finite resource. We are taught that degrees of success are finite. Maybe these things haven't been directly communicated to you, but we were all raised with a clear understanding of what jobs would be "good for us" or what lifestyle qualifies as "luxurious."

As a kid, I remember thinking if I saved $100, I'd be something. $100 felt like 1 million back then. When my family ate at McDonald's, we ordered off the dollar menu because "it was cheaper." Forget the dollar menu, CAN YOU IMAGINE how many happy meals you could buy with 1 million dollars?! I had big dreams.

As I grew closer to graduation, my parents suggested that I get into nursing because it pays well and there's job security. After all, what more could someone want from a career?

I am absolutely *not* a person that has a desire to work in a hospital or in the medical field. I am very grateful we have people that want to do that. In fact, my partner is going to be a nurse. But it wasn't for me.

So, they suggested government work. If I could work for the city, state, or federal government, I'd have stable benefits, solid pay, and permanent job security. I took the route suggested, joined the military at seventeen years old and turns out, they were right. The pay is comfortable; I have health benefits, a retirement account, and pretty good job security. But this isn't where I am at my best and it's definitely not where I am my happiest possible self.

When this realization came, I began working through my own 5D process, outlining exactly what I wanted out of my career and my life. What would make me the best, most successful, enriched, and empowered version of myself? The answer? Coaching.

So here I am, working to empower LGBTQ+ entrepreneurs just like you. My passion is putting more money in the hands of folks just like you. And yes, I'll need to keep working for the government while I make it happen, but I'm well on my way and so are you!

Recognize that we *all* were taught to believe there is not enough money to go around. You are not alone on this journey of undoing.

It will be difficult at times. As queer folk, we still face systematic hurdles and barriers that become even more prevalent when we look at intersectionalities between race and gender identity. But there **are** examples of people who have gone out and done it before us to prove it's possible.

One of my role models is Arlan Hamilton of Backstage Capital. If you don't know her, put a bookmark in this book right now and go Google her. Arlan is an amazing Black, queer woman who created a venture capital firm from nothing because the white dudes wouldn't let her in. She sidestepped and made her own company and has since invested millions into companies owned by people of color, women, and LGBTQ+. She's an amazing example of resilience and laser focus. She is sure to inspire you to go after what you want out of your life.

Whether you have an idea for a business or are currently running a business but not making much money, know you are an inspiration. Just by chasing what you want, you are giving other queer folk permission to do the same.

Defining *Audacity*

If you're like me, when you hear the word *audacity*, you think of the sheer entitlement of white, cis, straight men. In *We Should All Be Millionaires* by Rachel Rodgers, Rachel explains why we all should have the confidence of a mediocre white man. The issue most of us face is a hard case of imposter syndrome. We belittle our successes and our skill sets until we become totally immobilized.

You know who *isn't* doing that? Cis, straight, white men. Mediocre men walk through the world as if it is all owed to them and they never look back.

You are different. You are going far beyond the bare minimum.

Nothing has been handed to you. You're going to go out and get it for yourself.

You are going to have the audacity to be bold.

So how do we keep the spark going?

Consistency. Refer back to your plan often, adjust, be flexible but **keep going.**

Internalize this plan as the new you, your new identity.

You ARE these new things. You ARE wealthy, abundant, successful, knowledgeable, giving, attractive, magnetic, and inspiring. Write new stories about yourself, soak them up, and watch the magic happen.

Have the audacity to get clear on what you want, build a path to the place you want to be, and have the utter gall to start walking.

BASTIAN DZIUK

Bastian Dziuk (he/him) helps queer entrepreneurs reach their potential in life and business. His experiences as a queer and trans man, his passion for helping others build businesses, along with his leadership skills gained in the U.S. Army have provided him with a unique ability to help other queer entrepreneurs. He is a certified coach through JRNI Life Coach Training, has earned a B.A. in Cultural Entrepreneurship from the

University of Minnesota, Duluth, and continues to serve in the Minnesota National Guard.

Bastian's mission is to help others build queer wealth through entrepreneurship. With wealth comes power. With power comes influential change. Additionally, he believes we should have the skills to create the life we want to live. He guides his clients as they intentionally create their dream life.

Bastian resides in the Twin Cities of Minnesota with his partner. Outside of coaching, you can find him devouring podcasts, reading self-development books, and having bonfires in good company at home.

Website: https://www.coachbastian.co/
Instagram: https://instagram.com/coachbastian.co
Email: Bastian@coachbastian.co

A NOTE TO OUR READERS

Dear One,

What did you think about this crazy book? Wild, right? Did you ever think you'd see an entire business book published by a queer press, and completely written by out and proud entrepreneurs? Me either.

But it's more than that. I didn't even **think** to look for it. It didn't enter my consciousness as I started my third business, my first business as an out lesbian. I never thought, "Maybe there's a book about how to get my mindset in the right space, written for me, by my people."

But even if I had, it wasn't there. There are a few books about creating inclusive workspaces. A few about the politics of business and the LGBTQ+ community. Even fewer on how to help your business position for access to the $3.3 trillion LGBTQ+ buying power.

But nothing really *from* us, *for* us.

And yes, we could have gathered a gaggle of queer celebrities and asked their assistants to write a chapter for them. After a year or so, we'd have *that* book. But that wasn't where my heart was pulling me.

We could have distilled MBA school down into fourteen chapters, slapped a rainbow on it, and called it good. But my heart said, "Hell no." All the business tools in the world won't make a difference if you are questioning your own validity.

I wanted to be able to feel like all of the authors were just. like. me. I wanted a book full of accessible experts. I wanted to feel like I could slide into any of their DMs, ask my burning questions, and actually get a response. I wanted to know, without a shadow of a doubt, that not only could the hot and trendy TikTok gays find success, but regular ole queers like me could too.

Frankly, I wanted to close this book feeling like I have fourteen new queer friends.

And you do. You are literally not alone.

We all hustlin', just like you. We're all trying to pay the bills through work that doesn't suck our souls from our bodies. We are all walking the walk.

Your next level is waiting. OUR next level is waiting.

And everything we need to get there, we already have. Within ourselves and within each other.

Fam, we just made history. Us by publishing this book, and you by purchasing and reading it. Our collective queer joy and success is an act of revolution.

Let's change the world.

Elena Joy Thurston
Founder of Pride and Joy Publishing

FIND OUT MORE

For more great books, please visit Pride & Joy Publishing online at
https://gracepointpublishing.com/pride-and-joy-publishing

PRIDE & JOY
publishing

FOOTNOTES

Foreword

1. The Out & Equal 2019 Workplace Equality Fact Sheet] link: https://outande-qual.org/2019wefs/
2. https://www.entrepreneur.com/article/363407
3. The New American Economy: https://www.newamericaneconomy.org/issues/entrepreneurship/

5. From Burn Out to Glow Up

1. Chinn, Juanita J., Martin, Iman K., and Redmond, Nicole. 2021. "Health Equity Among Black Women in the United States." *Journal of Women's Health*, Vol. 30, 2. https://www.liebertpub.com/doi/10.1089/jwh.2020.8868
2. Lean In. "Black Women aren't Paid Fairly, and that Hits Harder in an Economic Crisis." n.d. https://leanin.org/data-about-the-gender-pay-gap-for-black-women#!
3. Comen, Evan. 2019. "The Worst Cities for Black Americans." 24/7 Wall Street. https://247wallst.com/special-report/2019/11/05/the-worst-cities-for-black-americans-5/4/
4. National Center for Education Statistics. "Degrees Conferred by Race and Sex." U.S. Department of Education, National Center for Education Statistics. (2019). *Status and Trends in the Education of Racial and Ethnic Groups 2018* (NCES 2019-038), Degrees Awarded. https://nces.ed.gov/fastfacts/display.asp?id=724
5. Van Wouwe, Jacobus P. (ed.) "Physical, psychological and occupational consequences of job burnout: A systematic review of prospective studies." *PLoS One.* 2017; 12(10) https://www.ncbi.nlm.nih.gov/pmc/articles/PMC5627926/

7. The Power of OPA!

1. https://blog.leeandlow.com/2020/01/28/2019diversitybaselinesurvey/

CPSIA information can be obtained
at www.ICGtesting.com
Printed in the USA
BVHW040045181021
619127BV00004B/14